Inside the Music

BY DAVE STEWART

Miller Freeman Books

San Francisco

Published by Miller Freeman Books
600 Harrison Street, San Francisco, CA 94107
Publishers of Keyboard, Bass Player, and Guitar Player magazines

un Miller Freeman
A United News & Media publication

Photo of John Thomson (in his Louis Balfour guise) courtesy of The Fast Show and B.B.C. TV. Great!

Distributed to the book trade in the U.S. and Canada by Publishers Group West, 1700 Fourth St., Berkeley, CA 94710

Distributed to the music trade in the U.S. and Canada by Hal Leonard Publishing, P.O. Box 13819, Milwaukee, WI 53213

Cover design: The Visual Group
Music typesetting and layout: Ernie Mansfield Music

Library of Congress Cataloging in Publication Data:
Stewart, Dave.
Inside the music : the musician's guide to composition, improvisation, and the mechanics of music / Dave Stewart.
      p.   cm.
     ISBN 0-87930-571-1
1. Music–theory 2. Composition (Music) 3. Improvisation (Music)
I. Title.
MT6.S785 1999
781–dc21   99-22676
                                     CIP

Printed in the United States of America
99 00 01 02 03 04   5 4 3 2 1

CONTENTS

*To Barb, my heavenly-voiced companion
and to The Inland Revenue, motivators sans pareil*

Introduction

My first book, *Introducing the Dots*, later reprinted as *The Musician's Guide to Reading & Writing Music*, first hit the streets in the early 1980s, causing a major litter problem and great embarrassment to my publishers. Since then, many kind folk have told me they found the book useful and 'unintimidating'. With these intrepid souls in mind, I am pleased to offer this somewhat belated follow-up.

Like its predecessor, this book aims to present the inner workings of music in a terror-free way. Where the first volume concentrated on the basics of reading and writing music, this one takes a wider view, with chapters on MIDI, composition and improvisation. The examination of chords and chord voicings initiated in the first book continues, along with further studies of chord sequences, rhythm, drumming, tempo and tonality, and a glossary of musical terms, signs and symbols. If you like, this is a slightly more advanced companion to my first offering—but really, both books have the same purpose: to throw some light on the terminology, written language and celestial mechanics of music, and (more importantly) to encourage readers not just to read music, but to write some of their own.

Permit me to interject a gripe here; there is a widespread perception that in order to be a musician, you have to be born with some God-given talent which differentiates you from other mortals. This strikes me as a rather silly, divisive idea—in my opinion, being a musician has less to do with talent than it does with the ability to respond to what you hear. Most people enjoy music; beyond that, learning the craft of music certainly involves a lot of hard work, and can take years. The 'talented' folk may master the basics quicker than most (or have more confidence to market themselves), but as far as creative music-making is concerned, the doors should be open to everybody.

If music is primarily an expressive emotional force, you might ask, why do we need to concern ourselves with its technicalities? Good question. Before it can be understood and dissected, music must be felt, but although it creates emotion, music is not made of feelings, but of notes, sounds and rhythm. These simple materials require organisation, and the more skill you can bring to bear on organising them, the more subtle and expressive your music will be. The acquisition of musical skill does not rely on owning a lot of equipment, but it does involve a certain amount of knowledge, some of which I hope you will find lurking in the following pages.

My personal study of music, idiosyncratic though it has been, has kept me occupied for thirty years, and I am happy to share what I have learned with anyone who cares to read on. In this book, I have tried to present not just the bare technical facts, but also the musical ideas that come with them. Above all, I have done my best to be clear and practical, which is possibly all any music writer can aspire to. If anything contained herein inspires someone to write a piece of music, the book will have been well worth writing . . . Okay, that's enough rambling preamble. Now, as they used to say in episodic fiction, read on!

—Dave Stewart
London, February 20, 1998

ONE

Intervals

One of my favourite authors, Anthony Burgess, had a habit of starting his novels with a rather impenetrable opening paragraph, as if to test his readers' commitment. My strategy, developed over years of writing music articles, is the opposite: I lull my readers into a false sense of well-being with a little amusing trivia, then, without warning, confront them with some horrible technical stuff about the effects of the augmented 11th on an E♭ dominant 13th chord. This abrupt switch of tone must have irritated thousands of casual browsers, but the faithful few who enjoy thinking about what makes music tick and who regularly tune in to follow my ravings will doubtless have grown used to it by now. In either case, here it is–my second book on music, kicking off with a chapter on pitch intervals.

That's the difficult opening paragraph out of the way, and it's all going according to plan–I open with a few chatty personal remarks, you're feeling comfortable and relaxed, when suddenly I hit you with a nasty-looking diagram:

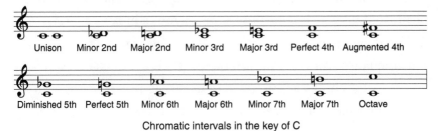

Chromatic intervals in the key of C

Aaaargh! This collection of symbols shows a series of ascending notes, all named in relation to a fixed lower pitch (or *root note)* of Middle C. The ascending notes rise in semitone steps, and we call the intervals they form with C *chromatic intervals* (from the Greek *chromatikos*, meaning coloured)–there are twelve semitones between Middle C and the C an octave above, with a halfway point of F♯ (G♭) six semitones up. If we omit all the intervals with 'minor' or 'diminished' in their name, the remainder (called 'major' and 'perfect') are the notes of the C major scale. (More of which later.)

These intervals occur frequently throughout this book; so, if any are unfamiliar to you, please take some time to get acquainted with their names and sound. I've used the note of C as a starting point for each interval, but the formula for naming intervals remains the same whatever the starting tone. For example, the interval between an E and an F♯ one tone higher is a *major 2nd*, and the interval between an E and a B seven semitones higher is a *perfect 5th*. A good working knowledge of intervals helps us understand how scales and melodies are constructed, how chords and chord voicings are created, how chord sequences are formed, and the larger relationships of musical keys. Twelve small steps to a large amount of knowledge!

Practice vs. Theory

You may be wondering why these interval names are necessary–isn't it enough just to know the names of the notes? Oddly enough, when daydreaming about music, I tend not to think in terms of 'minor 6ths' and so on. Often, I just visualise some notes laid out on a keyboard, and my musical memory supplies the right sound (and the feeling that comes with it) without my having to name the notes. But when discussing music with others (such as yourself, dear reader) it becomes necessary to revert to names and terms in order to communicate musical ideas. So my advice would be twofold: learn the interval names, but link the names with the sound and shape of the interval on your instrument—that way, you'll be in full control of both the theory and the practice.

The Perfect 5th

If you only have time to memorize one interval from the set shown above, let it be the perfect 5th. When played in conjunction with the root note, the perfect 5th has an amazingly strong, simple and natural sound that no other interval can rival. For that reason, the perfect 5th is the foundation of all basic chord construction. Here is a selection of perfect 5ths in various keys:

Key of C   Key of F   Key of G   Key of A   Key of D   Key of E   Key of B   Key of B♭

Sometimes, especially with certain electronic sounds, the root and 5th combine so completely that it is hard to tell we are actually hearing two pitches—a good example of this are rock guitar 'power chords': played in 5ths low down on the neck with amp distortion, they sound like one huge note.

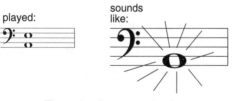

The rock guitar power chord

The Major 3rd

When added to a root note and perfect 5th, the major 3rd completes the *major triad.* (Minor triads are made by using the minor 3rd.) By cultural consensus, major triads sound positive and cheerful, whereas minor triads are taken as sad and reflective. Funny how shifting just one note changes the mood completely . . .

strongly both to each other and to their root note, and play a large part in governing the construction of chords and chord sequences.

The Perfect 4th

If you *invert* the interval of a perfect 5th (that is, drop the upper note of the 5th down an octave so it falls *under* the root rather than above it), you get a perfect 4th. 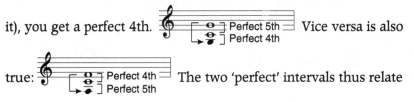 Vice versa is also true: The two 'perfect' intervals thus relate

Equal Temperament

(*A short treatise on instrument tuning for those who are interested in scientific facts.*)

In physical terms, doubling a note's frequency makes it sound an octave higher, so if we adopt the widespread convention of tuning the A above Middle C to 440 cycles per second, the A above it will be 880 cycles, and the A below it 220 cycles.

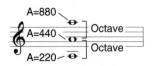

Working out the semitones' tuning is less straightforward—here, the magic number is 1.0594631, the 12th root of 2. If we multiply a given frequency by this number 12 times, we end up with a frequency

double what we started with, and the intervening 12 steps will all have the same frequency ratio to their neighbours. By this calculation, we can therefore divide the octave into twelve equidistant semitones. This system of tuning is called *equal temperament*, and it has become the norm for most commercially produced acoustic and electronic musical instruments.

It was not always so. Prior to the 19th century, instruments were tuned to pure mathematical ratios, which actually produce a more satisfying sound—untempered major 3rd and perfect 5th intervals, a little flatter and sharper respectively than their equally tempered versions, sound rich and glorious when combined in chords with their root note. But the problem was that this glorious sound could be heard only in a limited number of keys—if you used the pure (i.e., slightly flat) major 3rd as the 5th step of a new key, its flatness made it sound out of tune. In order to eradicate such tuning difficulties, equal temperament was pioneered by a number of 18th century German composers, including J. S. Bach. Though some purists find the equal temperament system an unacceptable compromise, its great advantage is that it enables us to move freely through all twelve keys, thereby creating infinite possibilities for harmonically adventurous composers.

TWO

Tonality/Simple Chord Sequences

A funny thing happens if you play a major chord for a while. Let's imagine that one afternoon, you find yourself in the Great Hall of your stately home, surveying your collection of rare musical instruments. Reaching for a clavichord or priceless Renaissance lute, you listlessly thrum the chord of C major for about 20 seconds. Instinctively, your hand slips up to the chord of F major (another easy one). From there, the short journey to G major is not too taxing, after which you run out of ideas and return to C major. How does it feel to be back in C major? In musical terms, it feels as though you have returned *home*. The feeling of home, that this is the place where the music might linger and finally come to rest, is called *tonality*.

The Tonic / (Sub)dominant Experience

I hope playing the chords of C, F and G on imaginary 16th-century instruments was as enjoyable for you as it was for me. As has been chronicled in countless music theory books, these three chords can be named in relation to each other:

C is the **tonic** chord, based on the tonal centre or **root** note,

F is the **subdominant** chord, based on the interval of the **perfect 4th** above the root, and

G is the **dominant** chord, based on the interval of the **perfect 5th** above the root.

Describing C as the 'tonal centre' is the same thing as saying that the music is in the key of C. The term 'dominant' is from the Latin word for 'leading', the idea being that the dominant chord leads back to the tonic. (It doesn't have to, but that's the convention.) 'Sub' means 'underneath', which helps us remember the subdominant chord's position one tone beneath the dominant. This simple trinity is the 'three-chord trick' on which 15 trillion pop songs are based.

In the unlikely event of your being unfamiliar with the concept, our next diagram shows the tonic, subdominant and dominant chords in four adjacent white-note keys (C, D, E and F):

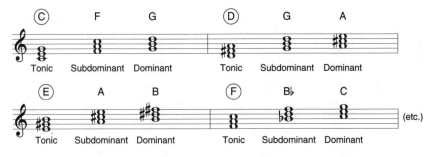

Learn this clutch of major chords starting on every semitone, and you can dominate the pop charts in all twelve keys.

Simple Chord Sequences

The 12-bar

The most profoundly simple songs are based around tonic, subdomi-nant and dominant chords:

A staggeringly simple chord sequence

Sequences may be 4 or 8 bars long, but one of the most common structures is the *12-bar.*

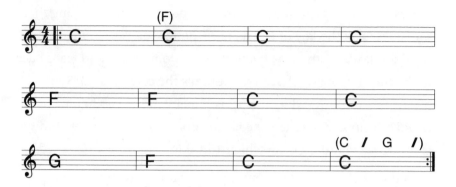

(Substitute the chords in brackets for a slightly more elaborate version.) The 12-bar is used extensively in blues, R&B and rock 'n' roll. If you want examples, Elvis Presley's 'Hound Dog' is a simple 12-bar, while Chuck Berry's 'Route 66', with its change up to the subdominant in the second bar, is based on the alternative version. The 12-bar is rock's common currency, and when musicians jam, this is very often the chordal structure they try to follow. Such jam sessions, once started, are difficult to end, so if you ever find yourself stuck in the middle of a 12-bar which threatens to go on for the rest of eternity, bring matters to a conclusion by playing this riff in bars 11 and 12:

I guarantee it'll bring the house down.

Relative Minors

Each major key has its own relative minor key a minor 3rd below it. The easiest way to find the relative minor is to count three semitones down from the root:

The sound of the major chord followed by its relative minor is the archetypal sound of '50s pop, but musicians never seem to tire of its effect. The theme music of 'Twin Peaks' features this major-to-minor, happy-to-sad movement, no doubt with all sorts of post-modern, iconic and ironic intentions—it's still the same old chord change, though!

To break up the monotony of the 3-chord trick, wily songwriters of limited chordal means substitute the relative minor for the major, as in this example:

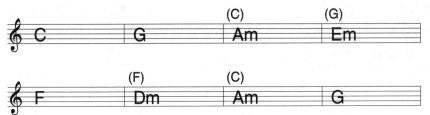

(Go ahead, steal it—I won't sue.) This is without doubt an improvement on the straight major version shown in brackets, but the effect is still pretty predictable—you've heard these changes a million times, and if you're anything like me, you'd be happy not to hear them again in yet another song. The problem with sticking to these six chords is that they are all based on the notes of the C major scale:

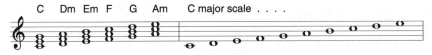

Harmonically speaking, this sets up a kind of static hum in the brain, which we have to be prepared to depart from at some point, or die of boredom. Fortunately, this departure came in the early '60s, when pop writers began to experiment wholesale with chord changes.

Breaking the Monotony

The break with 3-chord tradition came when groups started using chord sequences like:

By moving down a tone from the tonic (i.e., C to B♭), these writers were introducing a new element to the scale (in technical terms, the minor 7th interval) which did not fit previously established major scale patterns. Once this step had been taken, the floodgates opened, and chord changes such as C major down to A♭ major, C major up to E♭ major and C major up to E major via D major became commonplace. Perhaps unconsciously, groups were now happy to vary the tonality of their music, and even a song in the key of C major could feature changes like:

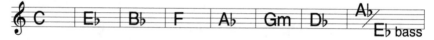

Whereas the old pop songs were rigidly *diatonic* (i.e., based on the notes of the key signature), the new kind (often pioneered by British bands, I'm proud to say) allowed temporary chromatic movements, such as C major to D♭ major. This is where, as a young musician listening to groups like The Who and the Jimi Hendrix Experience, I got interested.

Simple Chords, Unexpected Movements

Although there will always be guitar bands who recycle the same old changes, others (XTC and Radiohead spring to mind) are more chordally liberated. For myself, I believe it is still possible to write fresh-sounding music using simple chords, but we have to be prepared to think chromatically and imaginatively, and not be afraid to change key when the mood takes us. The following extract from the song 'As Far As Dreams Can Go' shows a simple but unusual chord sequence:

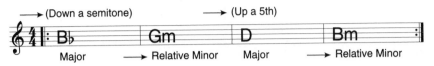

Though based on the classic schmaltzy pop movement of major to relative minor (which happens twice!), it features an unusual semitone change from B minor down to B♭ major. Another slight twist appears in the verse of 'My Scene':

Extract from 'My Scene'

There is nothing revolutionary about the movement from A♭ major to E minor over G bass, but it is quite an unexpected chord change for a pop song!

I particularly like the effect of this simple chordal movement:

Placing the second chord's 3rd in the bass means that although the chord goes down, the bass line moves up! You can see an expanded version of this in this extract from the chorus of 'New Jerusalem':

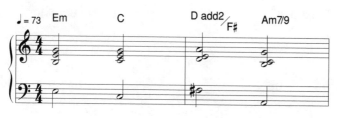

Extract from 'New Jerusalem'

These two bars mix basic triads with slightly more complex chords. In later chapters we'll examine the construction of these more elaborate voicings–'yuppie chords', as someone once called them–in some detail.

(More complex chord sequences may be found in Chapter Thirteen, under 'Composing with Chords'.)

THREE

Scales & Modes

An unfortunate byproduct of 20th-century Western music education is that in every musician's mind, scales are synonymous with pain. Physical pain—several of my musical colleagues tell of piano lessons in which their teacher rapped them across the knuckles with a ruler when they made a mistake. (Try that with me, and the pain would be swiftly reciprocated.) Mental pain—the torture of knowing you must spend eight hours a day for the rest of eternity practising scales so you can be a 'good' musician.

What a lot of crap. Music is not about pain, it is about the organisation of sound into an expressive emotional force. That said, this organisation cannot be achieved without a certain amount of knowledge and discipline. Even the most lowly punk musician must learn at least one chord, and accept the discipline that it must not be thrashed mercilessly until some time after the shout of 'One! Two! One, two, three, four!' If we want to take music a step further, we may find ourselves considering chordal harmony, and that will inevitably lead us to think about the notes of the scale. If, for example, we play a G major 7th chord, we have to know that the major 7th note in the G major scale is F♯, and that if the chord were G dominant 7th, the 7th would become the note F. Similarly, a jazz saxophonist must know which notes of the scale work in conjunction with an A13 augmented

11 chord in order that he can fit his improvised melodies with the pianist's backing.

In this chapter, I've selected some scales which I have found to be useful in improvisation and composition. I've followed the convention of presenting them in the key of C, not because of any personal leanings towards that note, but because it is a key that many musicians know well. Do not feel obliged to 'practise' these scales in the sense of endlessly running up and down them as if they were a bunch of musical stepladders—that may be good exercise for the fingers, but it's your brain I'm really interested in. However, do think hard about the intervals found in the scales, and listen to how they sound subtly different from one another.

Heptatonic (7 note) Scales

Here are five commonly found scales with a major 3rd. The first, the definitive C major scale, contains all major and perfect intervals (reckoning C as the lower note of each interval); the other scales are variants which flatten or sharpen certain notes.

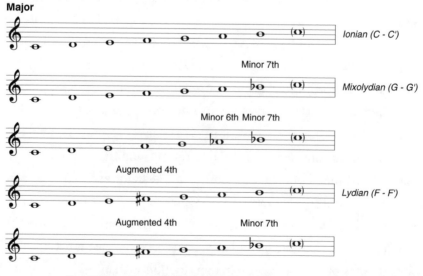

Five common 7-note **Major scales** (key of C)

Flattening the 3rd of the scale makes it minor. Conventional music theory promotes the notion of two forms of the 'melodic minor' scale, one for ascending melodies, the other for descending. I see little point in perpetuating this practice—having gone up in the elevator, I prefer not to come down by the stairs—so here the two melodic minor forms are presented as different scales, both of which could be used going up or down! The 'harmonic minor' scale combines a minor 6th with a major 7th interval, creating a wide gap of three semitones, which is marked.

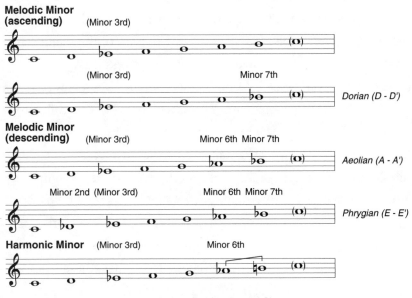

Five common 7-note **Minor scales** (key of C)

The next two scales flatten the 2nd to create a semitone as their first step. The first scale is technically major, but its pair of wide intervals give it an Arabic quality. The second scale uses a flattened (diminished) 5th interval, which makes it a little awkward compositionally—it would sound quite dissonant played over a C minor chord, for example. I include it to complete the modes (see below).

Two 7-note scales using the **Minor 2nd**

Modes

A music critic once innocently pointed out that a Beatles tune used the Mixolydian mode, and the screams of laughter still reverberate. What the poor man meant was that the lovable but filthy rich Liverpudlians were deliberately flattening the 7th of the major scale, but that would probably have been deemed no less hilarious. Anyway, what is a 'mode'? It's no big deal—modes are scales based on the white notes of the keyboard. The scale from C to C is called the Ionian mode, the scale from D to D (which is a minor scale) the Dorian mode, and so on. (The names are taken from ancient Greek tribes.) In early church music, these modes were used by composers to set the mood of the piece, along with a few rules about what note to finish on and so forth. Apparently, if you wanted to vary the last note of a piece, the mode had to be given a new name (such as the 'Hypophrygian'), but I don't want to get into all that—these rules were set too long ago to have any current relevance.

All seven white note modes appear in my scale examples above, but because my scales are in the key of C, all the modes but the Ionian have been transposed from their original key. If you take the Aeolian mode (A to A) as an example, you will understand that its original pitches of A, B, C, D, E, F and G have to be refigured as C, D, E♭, F, G, A♭ and B♭ to sound right in the key of C. Got it?

Whole Tone (6 note) Scale

Dividing the octave into six equal steps gives us the *whole tone* scale, beloved of Debussy and others. There are only two whole tone scales, shown below. Without semitones (or perfect 5ths) to give us a map reference, music written exclusively in the whole tone scale sounds tonally vague, though very beautiful.

The 6-note **Whole Tone** scale

Pentatonic (5 note) Scales

Much folk music is written in a 5-note *pentatonic* scale, based on the root, major 2nd, major 3rd, perfect 5th and major 6th intervals. (In other words, the major scale with its 4th and 7th omitted.) A minor version (actually the same scale transposed up a minor 3rd) uses the root, minor 3rd, perfect 4th, perfect 5th and minor 7th. The blues scale is basically a pentatonic minor scale with the anguished 'blue note' of a flattened 5th (in the key of C, G♭) added.

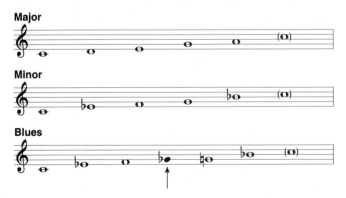

The 5-note **Pentatonic** scale

Alternating Tone/Semitone (8 note) scale

Although the following scale might seem to fall into the 'completely useless/hopelessly academic' category, I know several compositions which employ it to stunning effect! The scale has only three possible keys:

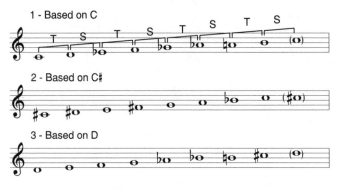

The 8-note **Alternating Tones/Semitones** scale

Please bear in mind that the scales shown above are only a brief selection from a virtually limitless collection of possibilities. A fellow called Busoni claimed to have found 113 7-note (heptatonic) scales, but the octave could be divided in many other ways, as you saw with the 8-note scale above. When you'd finally finished carving up the octave into all its possible intervallic combinations, you could start devising scales that spanned 24 semitones, with different pitches in the upper and lower octaves!

(Turn to the appendix for a brief analysis of Indonesian scales.)

FOUR

Chords & Chord Voicings I

It is possible to play perfectly good music without using chords, but well chosen chord voicings have such a powerful emotional effect on the listener that it is hard to see why anyone would willingly forgo them. While some rock and pop musicians happily get by with only a handful of simple chord shapes, I'm sure there are many others who would like to expand their harmonic vocabulary without resorting to the dreaded 'jazz chords'. In the next five chapters, I'll show you some useful chords and chord voicings which liven up the basic triad, but avoid sleazy jazz clichés.

Most of the chord books I have seen attempt to teach the subject by what I call the 'balancing donuts' method. In this, more and more thirds are piled on top of a basic triad until teetering monstrosities

like are created. Although this chord is logically con-

The 'balancing donuts'

structed, it sounds bloody horrible, and its name alone—C7/9/#11/13 —is enough to put anyone off chords for life. I prefer a more open approach to chord voicing, with a less rigid method of introducing exotic harmonic elements. Let's start with some fairly simple chords, and look at their voicing possibilities.

(Guitarists please note—guitar chord voicings are for 6-string guitar in conventional E, A, D, G, B, E tuning. Unplayed strings are marked x, open strings o, 'T' means play with thumb. It is not always possible for a guitar to play my examples, but where possible I've included a guitar shape which will cover at least the higher notes of the chord. In my experience, keyboards and guitars usually end up playing different voicings of chords anyway, so a little divergence is no bad thing.)

Suspended 4th Chords

A suspended 4th (or 'sus 4') chord is created by omitting the third from a triad and replacing it with a perfect fourth.

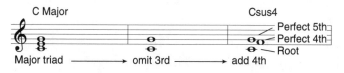

As the name suggests, this produces a feeling of slight harmonic suspense, which can be resolved by returning to the original triad.

 A somewhat sadder effect is produced by resolving a suspended 4th chord with a minor triad:

(Alternatively, you could sustain the fourth indefinitely and keep your listeners in suspense for the rest of their lives.)

Here are the three simplest voicings of the sus 4 chord:

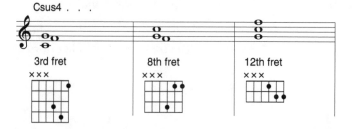

The chord can be strengthened by adding the octave:

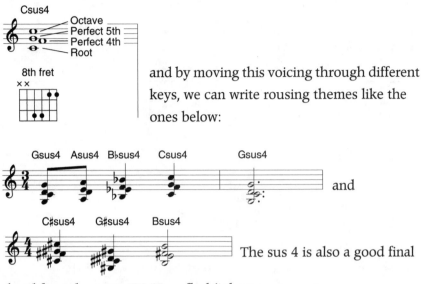

and by moving this voicing through different keys, we can write rousing themes like the ones below:

and

The sus 4 is also a good final chord for a dramatic TV 'Newsflash!' theme:

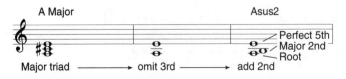

If you played the same thing using a straight A major chord, the mood would be much too happy.

With no third in its makeup, the sus 4 chord is neither major nor minor, but this ambiguity, coupled with its bold and simple nature, makes it a very useful chord indeed.

Suspended 2nd Chords

A close relative (and sometimes, identical twin) of the sus 4, the suspended 2nd (or 'sus 2') chord is made by dropping the third from a triad and substituting a major second:

This 3-note chord comes in three basic varieties:

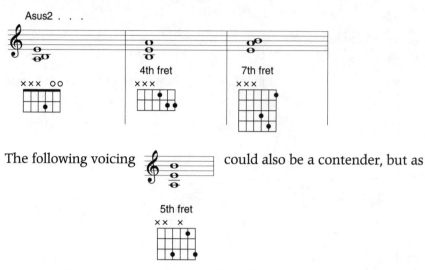

The following voicing 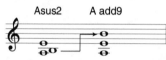 could also be a contender, but as

the second has been placed above the fifth at the top of the chord, it would be more correct to call it an added 9th (or 'add 9') chord.

(You could argue that, with no 3rd, it should be called a 'suspended 9th', but I've never heard anyone use that term.)

Like the sus 4, the sus 2 has a strong, simple sound and is neither major nor minor. Sliding from straight triads to suspended 2nds and back again has a nice effect:

In conjunction with the sus 4, the suspended 2nd can be used to generate jangly pop guitar intros like this one:

Guitar shapes:

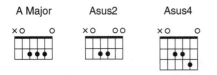

A Major   Asus2   Asus4

This style has been used by guitarists since the beginning of time (well, the '60s at least), usually in the keys of D, G or A to take advantage of the guitar's open strings. On a historical note, I believe it was originated by British Merseybeat group the Searchers, then borrowed by U.S. 12-string janglers the Byrds. Rekindled by the Pretenders and now recycled by legions of '90s guitar groups, this sort of simple movement still has charm, and is a good example of how the use of passing notes (i.e., the 2nd and 4th) can add harmonic and rhythmic interest to a plain major triad.

The Name Game

I've enjoyed clarifying these two chord names, but now I'm going to confuse you again. Look at this chord: . Earlier, I told you it was the third voicing of A sus 2, but is it not also E sus 4 in its basic position? Yes, I'm afraid it is. Depending on context and the choice of bass note, the same chord could be given two different names. With an A in the bass, it would be A sus 2:

Asus2

, but with an E bass note it becomes E sus 4:

Esus4

(With an F or F# in the bass it would change identity again, but more of that later!) The change of bass note gives the chord quite a different character, so a change of name is musically appropriate. If you ever find yourself becoming confused by these ambiguities, try to be clear in your mind about the three elements which make up a triad:

The **root**, which is the note name of the chord.

The **third**, which determines whether a chord is major or minor.

The **perfect fifth**, which combines with the root to give a chord sonic strength.

These are the important notes to look for in any chord, the fundamentals to which more exotic intervals (2nds, 4ths, 6ths, 7th, 9ths, etc.) are added. Any of the three may be omitted from a chord voicing as the composer desires, but when present, they have a powerful effect on a chord's sound. After a while, you will begin to recognise their effect, and that's when you will be able to name chords just by hearing them. This is not a trick or a special skill, just a question of familiarity.

Returning to our A sus 2 chord, you will notice that it consists of the two fundamental notes A and E (root in octave position and 5th respectively) to which a top note of B (the 2nd or 9th) is added.

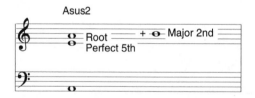

In the E sus 4 chord, the same notes are doing different jobs: The strong notes of E and B (root and 5th respectively) now frame the chord, and the 4th (A) is added a tone under the top note.

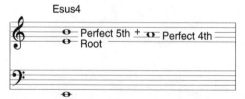

The doubling of the chords' roots in the bass reinforces their tonality, and should leave us in no doubt about what to call them!

FIVE

Chords &
Chord Voicings II

Added 4th Chords

Take a major triad. Do not shake or stir. Warm slightly and serve
with a sprinkling of added intervals, in this case a perfect 4th:

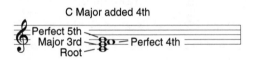

These ingredients make a tasty and nourishing chord which is a
close relative of the sus 4, but with the 3rd present too, we should
call it C major added 4th or 'C add 4'. This chord retains the positive
quality of the major triad, but the addition of the 4th creates extra
jangle in the sound. The four examples which follow show simple
keyboard voicings of a C major add 4 chord, and guitarists can sample the flavour by playing the last two:

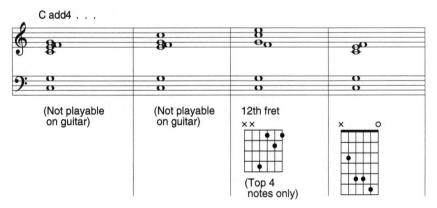

If you want wider intervals in the chord, spread your fingers and try this version:

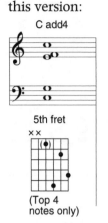

C add4

5th fret
(Top 4 notes only)

The minor version also sounds effective:

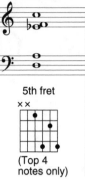

Cm add4

5th fret
(Top 4 notes only)

Added 2nd/9th Chords

A perfect 2nd (or perfect 9th, which is the same note an octave higher) may also be added to a major triad without omitting the third. The resulting 4-note chord is called the added 2nd (or added 9th), and like the added 4th chord above, it offers a way of extending a major triad without compromising its positive atmosphere.

The most basic voicing of the add 2 chord contains a small 'cluster' of adjacent notes consisting of the root, perfect 2nd and major 3rd:

G Major   G Major added 2nd

Major triad   +   Major 2nd   =   Perfect 5th
                                       Major 3rd
                                       Major 2nd } Cluster
                                       Root

If we keep the chord's four notes adjacent, the four possible voicings are:

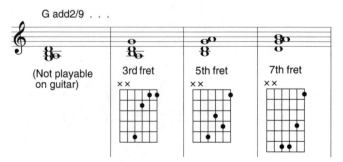

G add2/9 . . .

(Not playable on guitar)   3rd fret   5th fret   7th fret

(*Health warning: The guitar voicings, though theoretically playable, include wide stretches which may be impossible for some players.*) For keyboardists, clusters are easy and fun to play (though, in general, near-impossible for guitarists), but for a more open sound, try these wider-spaced voicings:

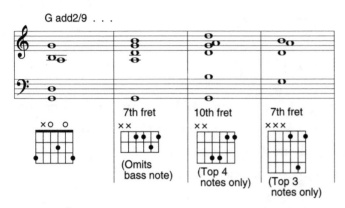

We can adopt the same procedure with a minor triad:

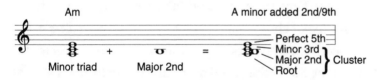

The four closest voicings for this chord are

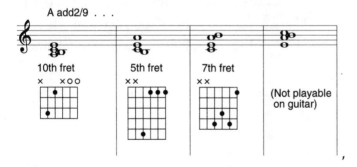

but wider voicings sound poignant and arguably more interesting, as these A minor add 2/9 chords demonstrate:

Am add2/9 . . .

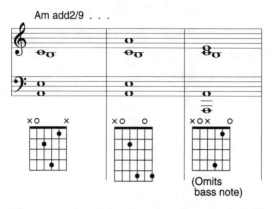

The second voicing is a good example of how a mixture of wide and narrow intervals can combine within a chord to create an attractive tension. (The intervals are, from the bottom up, A to E–perfect 5th, E to B–perfect 5th, B to C–semitone, C to A–major 6th.)

Added 2nd/9th Chords with 3rd in the bass

With its extra ingredient, the added 2nd/9th makes a pleasant alternative to a straight major chord, but changing its bass note makes it even more evocative. To my ears, one of the most exciting effects is produced when the 3rd of the chord drops down into the bass:

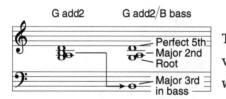

This leaves a less cluttered upper voicing of root, 2nd and 5th, which can be voiced as follows:

G add2/B bass . . .

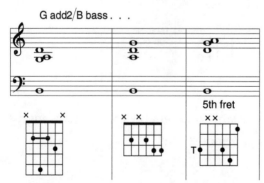

Doubling the 5th an octave higher gives a more triumphant sound:

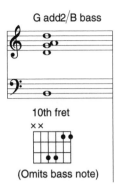

G add2/B bass

10th fret

(Omits bass note)

and in the following wide voicing, the four notes of the chord are distributed with near-equal intervals:

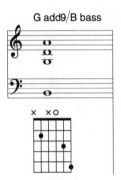

G add9/B bass

(Intervals from bottom up: B to G—minor 6th, G to D—perfect 5th, D to A—perfect 5th.)

As you have already guessed, we can do all this with a minor 9th chord too—here are the minor equivalents, in the key of A (I'm deliberately varying the key so you don't get bored):

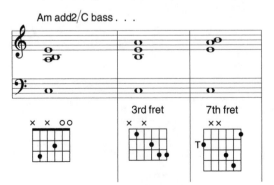

Am add2/C bass . . .

3rd fret   7th fret

A couple of triumphant-sounding wide voicings of the same:

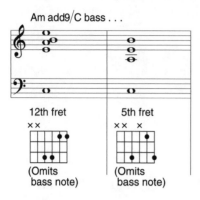

In a different context, some people might look at the bass note of the last voicings and describe them as some sort of C chord. That would be okay, but it would be a C chord with a 6th (A), a major 7th (B), but no 5th—there is no G in the chord. All three triadic elements of A minor (root—A, minor 2nd—C and 5th—E) are present, so in the name stakes, A minor technically beats C major by a short head. As A minor is the relative minor key of C major, we shouldn't be surprised by these close relationships!

Major 7/9 Chords

Major 7th chords consist of a major triad with an added major 7th interval. I like to voice major 7ths with a 5th in each hand, then add a 2nd or 9th:

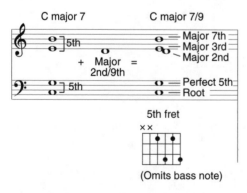

This gives us a major 7/9 chord with a bright, lush sound. In most keys, guitarists have to omit the bass note, but the full version is possible in the key of A:

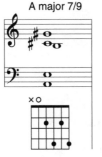

A major 7/9

If you find that voicing too bright, try this one, which has a sterner quality:

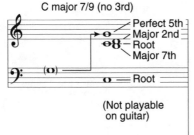

C major 7/9 (no 3rd)

Perfect 5th
Major 2nd
Root
Major 7th

Root

(Not playable on guitar)

The last chord has no 3rd, and in recent years, I have felt inclined to omit the 3rd from my original voicing, leaving these four notes:

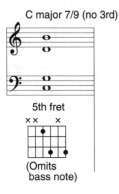

C major 7/9 (no 3rd)

5th fret

(Omits bass note)

I still think of this chord as a major 7/9, even though the absence of the major 3rd means it is technically neither major nor minor! You can see it at work in this extract from the song 'Shadowland':

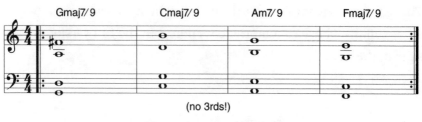

(no 3rds!)

Extract from 'Shadowland'

Major 7/9 Chords with 3rd in the Bass

Placing the 3rd in the bass of a major 7/9 chord creates a voicing which keyboardists and guitarists can both enjoy:

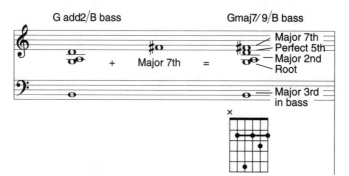

Hey—now we're *balancing donuts!* Looking at this from a keyboardist's perspective (hard not to, I've been playing the bloody things for 30 years), we can redistribute the notes of the chord so the LH plays a minor 6th interval consisting of the 3rd in the bass (B) and the root above it (G), while the RH plays what amounts to a D major triad (A, D & F♯).

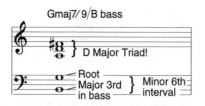

The D major business could lead to all sorts of arguments about the name of this chord, but always remember: MUSIC IS AMBIGUOUS. Having determined the correct name ('G major 7/9 over B bass' works

for me) after an unpleasant shouting match and a brief bout of fisti-
cuffs, we can generate a fair bit of musical electricity by shifting the
chord into different keys:

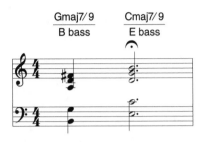

As we still have spare digits on our left hand, why not thicken the
chord by doubling the major 7th an octave down?

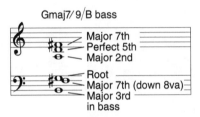

As the major 7th was already present, this has no effect on the name
of the chord, but adding a semitone to the LH changes the chord's
atmosphere in a subtle but unmistakable way. If you like the sound
of this 6-note voicing, it would be worthwhile to learn it in all 12
keys—as a keyboard exercise, try to play the shape in ascending semitones till you arrive at the octave.

Play this voicing in ascending semitone steps!

I guarantee you will make some mistakes the first time you try it, but
chordal mistakes can be interesting and profitable—if you accidental-
ly find another intriguing voicing en route, be sure to write it down
so you can remember it later! Once you're familiar with this voicing

in a number of different keys, you can use it to compose nice chordal movements like:

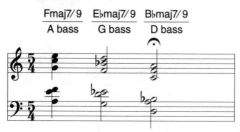

With five different pitches, each of which could appear (in theory) in three or four different octaves, there are 14,892,628 possible voicings of a major 7/9 chord with the third in the bass. Here are three more:

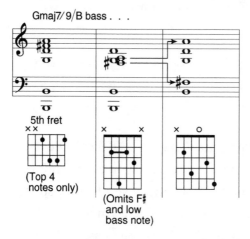

It is generally difficult for a guitar to cover all the component notes within one voicing, but the fortuitous open G string makes at least the last one playable! (Only in that key, though. . . .)

Although the second and third voicings share the same name, their effect is quite different. Whatever adjectives we use to describe it, the difference in sound is tangible, and illustrates the limitations of using abbreviated chord names like 'G major 7/9 over B bass'. If you want to maintain the particular musical mood that certain voicings create, you'll have to write them out in full notation.

'Shadowland' recorded by Dave Stewart & Barbara Gaskin, © Dave Stewart / Budding Music. All rights reserved.

SIX

Chords & Chord Voicings III

Dominant 7th Chords with Added 4ths

I have to confess at this point that I have an aversion to straight dominant 7th chords, which, as readers of my first book will recall, are created by adding a minor 7th interval to a major triad. I have tried various therapies to cure this allergy, including sitting within a few feet of a trad jazz group as they played a tune consisting entirely of dominant 7th chords. That took every ounce of my courage, but I still can't stand the sound—one reason might be that in its basic form, the chord is made up entirely of 3rds:

6th fret

The dreaded
dominant 7th
chord

Those bland old balancing donuts again. Fortunately, I have found a way of coping with my phobia—when confronted by a dominant seventh, I mess it up by slipping in a 4th, thereby breaking up the row of symmetrical intervals. Here's a nice voicing of a 7th add 4 chord which for some reason reminds me of '60s psychedelia:

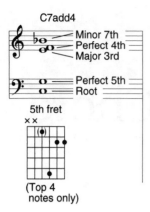

Not a 3rd interval in sight, though if we redistribute the notes in a cunning fashion we can end up with a pair of voicings made entirely of 4ths (though not all of them perfect):

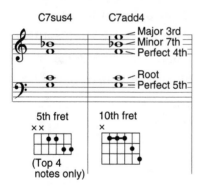

(The first voicing omits the 3rd, so is called '7 sus 4' rather than '7 add 4'.) Don't be confused by the term 'minor 7th' in the second chord's interval list—the presence of a major 3rd makes this a major chord, even though it contains a minor 7th interval.

Minor 7th Chords with Added 4ths

Minor 7th chords—now that's a different matter. Although they are now in danger of being over-used in soul and dance music (that dreadful house piano break doesn't help, either), minor 7th chords have the advantage of being capable of arrangement as a pair of perfect 5ths:

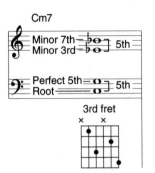

If we add a fourth to that, an extremely pleasant chord called the 'minor 7th add 4' emerges:

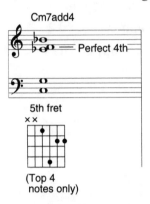

The flattening of the 3rd means we could now voice the chord as a row of four perfect 4ths:

but its true mystical nature is perhaps better expressed by these three voicings:

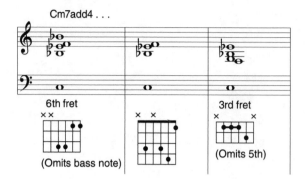

Cm7add4 . . .

6th fret
(Omits bass note)

3rd fret
(Omits 5th)

Minor 11th (Minor 7/9/11) Chords

As a rule of thumb, if you want to make a chord sound more interesting, put a 2nd or 9th in it. Adding a 2nd to our minor 7th add 4 chord adds poignancy, as well as introducing a nice jangly cluster in the heart of the chord:

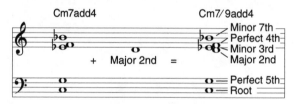

Cm7add4 + Major 2nd = Cm7/9add4

Minor 7th
Perfect 4th
Minor 3rd
Major 2nd
Perfect 5th
Root

Although by now our abbreviated chord names are beginning to get a trifle long-winded, I would call this chord 'C minor 7/9 add 4'. This full voicing has such a rich sound, we could compose whole songs round it; here are two bars to start you off:

Cm7/9add4   Fm7/9add4   Gm7/9add4

Things get even better—by the simple means of raising the 4th an octave so it becomes an 11th, we can create this superb minor 11th voicing, one of my all-time favourites:

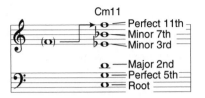

Guitarists can hear the effect of the 4th rising to the top of the voicing by playing this pair of chords:

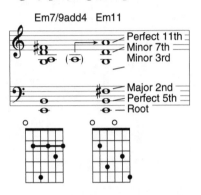

Notice how the latter voicing consists of two pairs of perfect 5ths connected by a semitone interval:

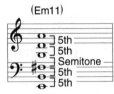

The elegant construction of wide and narrow intervals gives the chord its power. Aided by two conveniently placed open strings, we can also play this voicing of A minor 11th (which omits the 5th) on the guitar:

I gave up playing the guitar seriously when I was seventeen, but chords like this make me want to take it up again. (Screams of 'please God, no!' from neighbours.) Hey—I can still remember 'House of the Rising Sun'! Anyone wanna hear it? (Dead silence.)

Major Chords with an Augmented 4th

When is a 4th not perfect? When it is augmented, meaning sharpened by a semitone. (If you consult the table of chromatic intervals in Chapter One, you will see the 'augmented 4th' to the right of its perfect companion.) This interval (known as a 'tritone' as it consists of three whole tones) is exactly half an octave, and in the old days, folks thought that it summoned the devil. Let's try it and see, shall we:

The tritone rides out

AAAAAAAAAAARGH!

Only joking! Though this interval has absolutely no satanic connotations for me, I must admit it does sound slightly anxious . . . nevertheless, it is possible to weave it into some quite beautiful chord voicings which would make the devil himself weep.

The following example shows a 9th chord (no 3rd) with an added augmented 4th, which resolves to a straight add 9th.

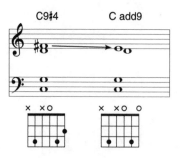

Once we have grown used to the sound of the first chord, we can sustain it and examine its intervals:

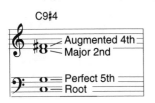

The 2nd seems to support the augmented 4th, and their pairing balances the low 5th at the bottom of the chord. We can strengthen the voicing by adding a 5th above the augmented 4th:

I used this chord, which seems to me to combine a sense of determination with a mystical quality, at the front of the Stewart/Gaskin track 'Levi Stubbs' Tears'. A guitar cannot play it in the key of C, but can manage it a minor 3rd down, in A:

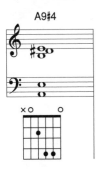

'Augmented 4th' is a bit of a mouthful, so jazz musicians, well known for their verbal terseness, have shortened the term to 'sharp 4th', which you will see written as '#4'. If only they were as succinct when it came to their solos. . . .

Major 7/#4 Chords

Having added a sharp 4th to a major chord, we can also add the major 7th:

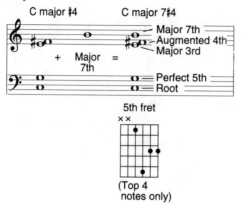

These two notes, a perfect 4th apart, seem to combine agreeably, which has the effect of softening the rather strained quality of the sharp 4th. The resulting 'major 7#4' voicing has something of a *film noir* atmosphere, as you will hear if you try this chordal movement:

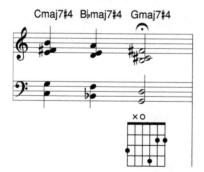

The chord also works well with the 5th omitted and the major 7th placed an octave lower, which gives guitarists a chance to play it in this shape:

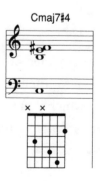

Major 7/9/#11 Chords

Having come this far, we can also add a 2nd or 9th to the chord, which makes a denser but still well-balanced sound:

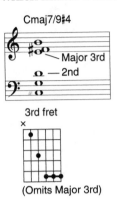

(Omits Major 3rd)

The coup de grace comes when we raise the sharp 4th an octave to become a sharp 11th:

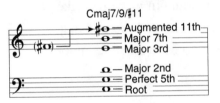

(Not playable on guitar)

I love this chord–if I had to take just one voicing with me to a desert island, this would be it. Like its minor 11th brother, it consists of two pairs of perfect 5ths separated by a narrow interval, in this case a tone.

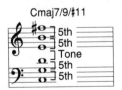

We can call this chord C major 7/9/#11, but its sound is the important thing–it has a yearning, heartfelt quality which sums up the power and mystery of music. It would be a shame if guitarists had no direct access to this chord, but there is a way—by detuning the bottom string a semitone to E♭, the voicing may be played as follows:

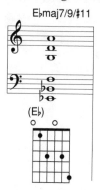

Major 7/6/9/#11 Chords

In our previous chord, the root, 2nd (or 9th), 3rd, 4th (or 11th), 5th and 7th are all represented in some form. The only note of the scale missing is the 6th, which we might as well put in for the sake of completeness! Starting with the all white-note chord of F major 7/9/#11, we can rearrange a couple of notes to make room for the new arrival:

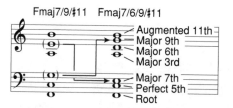

The guitar's version of this 7-note chord has to omit the 5th (only 6 strings, remember?), but sounds practically identical:

On guitar, the full version of this chord can be played only in the key of E, but guitarists (how can I put this politely?) will feel quite at home there.

With all seven notes of the scale included, the possible voicings of this chord would fill a book on their own, but here's one I particularly enjoy:

(not playable
on guitar)

This places the major 3rd in the bass, and the 5th and 6th side by side as nature intended. A reduced, more guitar-friendly shape omits both 5th and 9th, leaving a more open 4-note chord which also sounds good with a variety of altered bass notes:

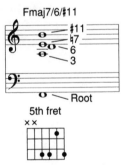

(Omits bass note)

SEVEN

Chords & Chord Voicings IV

In my first book, I was very rude about 6th chords, labelling them 'bland', 'greasy' and so forth. (I was very drunk, I mean very young, at the time.) Now I am older and more sober (sorry, I mean wiser), here is a chapter featuring, for the most part, chords characterised by the addition of the 6th (or 13th). I suspect this is the interval people have in mind when they sneer about 'jazz chords', and I sympathise with this viewpoint—on the other hand, I don't want to impose my taste on you, so please read on, check out these chords and make up your own minds!

Dominant 7/6/9/#11 Chords

Don't panic—this is simply a version of the previous chapter's last chord type with the 7th flattened by a semitone. The full guitar version (awkward to play on that instrument) illustrates the change well:

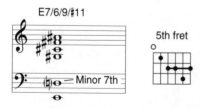

In this particular voicing, flattening the 7th has a fairly subtle effect, but the special character of the chord becomes more obvious when we return to the key of C and voice the chord without a 5th as follows:

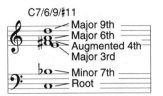

(Not playable on guitar)

This combination of tones excited the Russian composer Scriabin, who wove them into a very similar voicing which he named 'the mystic chord':

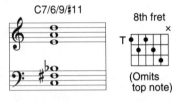

Alexander Nikolayevich
Scriabin's 'mystic chord'

Dominant 7/9/♯11 Chords

Believe it or not, the object of chord voicing is not to cram every note imaginable into a chord—the most effective voicings often involve only three or four notes. Having peaked with a couple of chords which cram all seven notes of the scale into some very full voicings, it's now time to start leaving a few notes out!

A useful chord is created by grouping the dominant 7th, 9th and ♯11th together over a single bass root note:

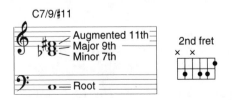

(Note the absence of both the 3rd and 5th.) You'll hear this simple but effective voicing used in Stevie Wonder songs and in countless jazz tunes, often as a means of moving away from a major chord:

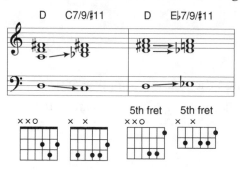

This voicing contains an interesting *double entendre*–taken alone, its upper three notes form an augmented chord.

Dominant 7/9/11/13 Chords

Flatten the 11th, add a 13th (which is the 6th an octave up), and you end up with a chord with a heavyweight name but a lightweight sound which is widely used in pop music. Like the previous voicing, this chord jettisons the 3rd and 5th. With no lower intervals to tie them down, the dominant 7th, 9th, 11th and 13th intervals combine to form a chord of their own which sounds almost independent of the underlying bass note. Let me show you what I mean:

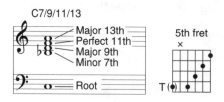

In this example, the notes Bb, D, F and A together constitute the chord of Bb major 7, but the addition of the C bass note places us in a tonal no man's land–we could call this chord C7/9/11/13, but it could equally well be seen as Bb major 7 over C bass. Either way, its ambiguous, sophisticated quality has endeared it to legions of soul balladeers, who weave it into chord sequences at every opportunity. This overuse may soon make this chord seem very stale, but it can be made to sound less trite by moving its top note down an octave:

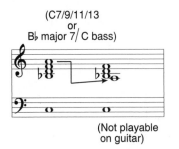

(Not playable
on guitar)

This gives it a tougher, more abstracted sound which suits angular chord sequences like this one:

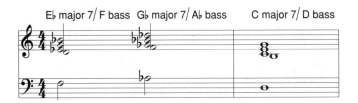

Dominant 7/9/13 Chords—the Jazz 13th

nice!

The chord with the scary name which jazz musicians use to spice up their tunes. (Or render them terminally bland, depending on your point of view.) In jazz harmony, a 13th chord is constructed by adding a high 6th (i.e., a 13th) to a dominant 7/9 chord:

(Omits bass note)

The 9th may be omitted, as follows:

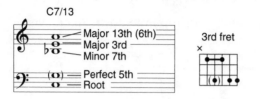

Because it has been used so much in the sort of jazz music you hear in elevators, I am afraid I now regard this chord as irretrievably sleazy, but the more open-minded reader might learn to love it.

A 13th chord (like most others) may be made minor by changing its major 3rd to a minor 3rd:

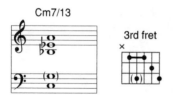

Though not quite as bland as the major version, it is still a sackable offence to use it in a mainstream rock or pop band.

Minor 7/11/13 Chords

Before we leave the stale, sleazy, sophisticated but smelly world of the jazz 13th, I should mention one more related chord which actually sounds really good to my ears. Here it is:

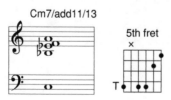

There is a strong argument for calling this some kind of F major chord (all three triadic elements —F, A and C—are included), but in the current context I'd settle for C minor 7 add 11/13. You can hear this chord blaring out at the front of a track called 'Mwamburi Dies Manfully' on Dirk Campbell's *Music from a Round Tower*, an album which I wholeheartedly recommend to lovers of harmonic and sonic exploration.

Major 7/6/9 Chords

The Major 7/6/9 is a fairly common jazz chord with an untroubled, relaxed sound—completely useless for punk rock. Its upper notes can be arranged as a row of three perfect 4ths, which suits the guitar:

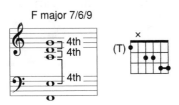

(In fact, now I think about it, this chord was probably invented by a guitarist.) Two alternative voicings follow, the second of which (with a mystical, bell-like sound) sounds great on a keyboard:

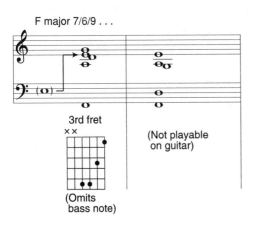

With the help of the open A string, guitarists can execute the latter in the key of A:

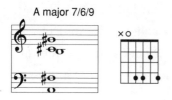

Major 6/9 Chords

A simple, 3-note chord with unfortunate connotations of 'easy listening' jazz. I personally find easy listening extremely hard work, but for those who want to sound jazzy, cool, relaxed, tanned and lightly amused while avoiding the bleeding fingers which come with augmented 11ths, this is the chord for you:

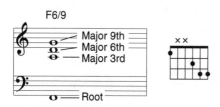

Guitarist's heaven—just a simple pair of 4ths, and let the bass player worry about that low note. Far be it from me to inject any angst, misery or despair into the proceedings, but there is a rather wretched sounding minor version:

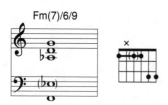

EIGHT

Chords & Chord Voicings V

Here follow a quartet of chord types each containing a flattened interval and likely to be constructed on a dominant 7th (as opposed to major 7th) model. This similarity apart, these chords have little in common, and each has its own distinctive atmosphere to contribute.

Flattened 2nd/9th (♭9) Chords

I first became fully aware of the flattened (or minor) 9th interval when I heard it blaring out at me under the line 'I don't mind' in the Beatles' mad song 'I Want to Tell You' (from *Revolver*). Later, I noticed chords with a minor second used in Chick Corea's Spanish-influenced compositions. The simplest construction of a flattened 2nd chord is as follows:

(In line with the policy adopted in Chapter Five, we should probably call it 'C add ♭2', but I've never heard anyone use that name!) A more elaborate version adds the minor (dominant) 7th interval and pushes the flat 2nd up an octave to the top of the chord:

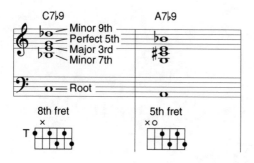

If we ignore the bass note, the four remaining intervals actually constitute a diminished 7th chord.

A more complex construction sees the minor 9th interval added to a 13th chord:

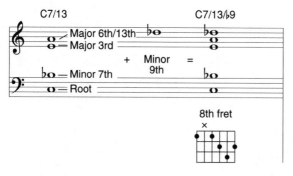

This voicing has bitonal tendencies (see below), and a sound which blends sophistication and hysteria. Its neurotic sound makes it seem desperate to resolve to another chord—any one.

Flattened 5th (♭5) Chords

This chord name is often used inaccurately. Sometimes an apparent flattened 5th is added to a chord, as in this C major 7 voicing:

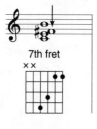

Flattened 5th or
Augmented 4th?

Unless you were looking for a spectacularly dissonant effect, you would be unlikely to include the perfect 4th in any accompanying melody. (Though a perfect 5th would sound reasonably harmonious.) To avoid the interval-name confusion of having a flattened 5th and perfect 5th in the same scale, it would be logical to call the added note an augmented 4th, and the chord C major 7♯4.

Adding a tritone to a minor 3rd does create a true flattened 5th:

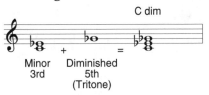

However, the convention is to call this a diminished chord. So does the ♭5 chord exist? I'm delighted to report that it does, and has recently been sighted in large numbers off the shores of Newfoundland. We can arrive at it by performing this musical equation:

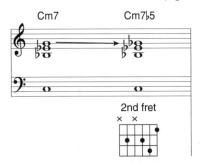

The result is a C minor 7♭5 chord, which might be accompanied melodically by the perfect 4th, diminished 5th and minor 6th intervals. (Or F, G♭ and A♭, as you and I prefer to call them.)

Flattened 6th (♭6) Chords

An agreeable way to squeeze a minor 6th interval into a chord is to add it to a major triad. I've selected a C major add 9 over E bass voicing (see Chapter Five) for this purpose:

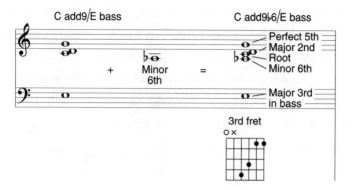

An alternative voicing places the minor 6th nearer the top of the chord, giving a more declamatory sound:

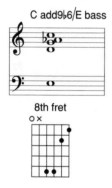

(*In the last two examples, the guitar bass note is an octave lower than written.*)

Though anxious not to create any confusion, I should point out that adding a minor 6th to a minor chord actually changes its tonality and name, as you can see in this example:

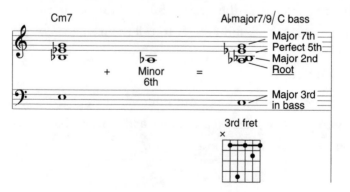

Technically speaking, this excellent chord has left the realms of C minor and become an A♭ major 7/9 chord (of the sort we saw in Chapter Five). My reasoning is that the A♭ major triadic elements (A♭, C and E♭) outweigh the C minor (C, E♭ and G), but this is probably getting too theoretical. It's a great chord—say no more.

Er—just one more small point. The minor 6th interval has a doppelganger called the augmented 5th, which you will see employed in augmented chords:

Flattened 10th (♭10) Chords

A stridently jazzy chord which was a favourite of Jimi Hendrix. (Check out the intros to 'Foxy Lady' and 'Purple Haze'—these jazz shapes sound much better played through a 200 watt Marshall stack.) Its interesting name stems from the fact that this unique dominant 7th chord contains both the major and minor 3rd, making it a sort of harmonic hermaphrodite. The minor 3rd is placed up the octave, making it a flattened 10th. (This still leaves the theoretical confusion of having two different thirds operating in one scale, so jazz musicians tend to call this chord a 'sharpened 9th' or '♯9'.)

The chord is constructed by adding a flattened 10th to a dominant 7th chord with no 5th:

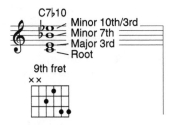

When I was 17, I used to love playing it on guitar (before the neighbours got up a petition) in this form:

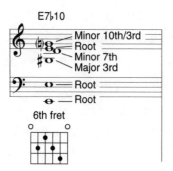

This must set a record for the most root notes in one chord—three of them appear in different octaves! It's a great shame Jimi Hendrix isn't still around, as I'm sure if he were he'd be contributing some wonderful guitar voicings.

We end our reasonably exhaustive examination of chords and their voicings with a miscellany which could be described as the 'X over Y' category.

Bitonal Chords

Some composers (Igor Stravinsky and Dirk Campbell spring to mind) like to simultaneously sound two triads in different keys, as with these compound chords:

The same thing can be done by superimposing minor chords, or by mixing majors and minors. I would recommend studying the score to the Introduction of 'Le Sacrifice' from Stravinsky's *Rite of Spring* to see this technique used in a masterly fashion. When the two chords are harmonically remote from each other (as in my examples), we can call the resulting concoction a 'bitonal chord', i.e. one which operates in two keys at once.

Chords with Altered Bass Notes

Sometimes I get tired of wrapping my brain round chord names like C7/9/♯11/13. Take the C13 ♭9 chord at the end of the 'Flattened 2nd/9th Chords' section above: rather than painstakingly working out each interval in relation to the root note, I might think of it as simply A major over C7. (The more so because I would play the A major triad with my right hand and the C7 notes with my left.) Similarly, I would probably call the following voicing 'E over C bass' rather than 'C major 7 augmented 5th':

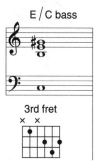

The argument over whether this is a bitonal chord is academic; the important thing is to know what the chord sounds like and be able to remember it!

I'll leave you with a couple of sequences which demonstrate the usefulness of 'X over Y bass' style chord names. The first shows a repeated minor chord with a simple descending bass line:

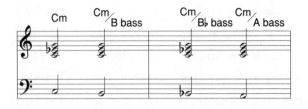

(You could call the last chord A minor 7 ♭5, but would that make life any easier?) My second example is a row of ascending triads (four major and one minor) with a contrary motion bass line:

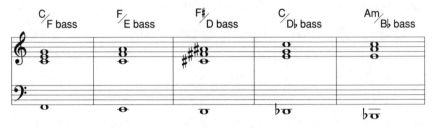

By my reckoning, only the third and fourth are bitonal, but all benefit from this clear and simple naming system.

NINE

Tempo

The jolly little signs we use to indicate rhythm $\left(\begin{array}{cccc} \flat & \downarrow & \downarrow & \overline{} \end{array} \right)$ tell us nothing about the speed of the music—that has to be defined by setting the *tempo* (Italian for 'time'). Nowadays we have pocket-sized electronic metronomes which display the tempo in b.p.m. (beats per minute), but in the old days, things were far less predictable. In a defiant display of player power, the musicians used to try to set the tempo themselves, with mixed results; the violinists, excited at the prospect of the concert ending early, would speed up, while the brass players, permanently befuddled by drink, would slow down. In order to reach the last chord together, the brass players had to be given a three-minute start.

Tick vs. Stick

In due course, the first clockwork metronomes were invented, but early models developed a limp at tempos under 70 b.p.m. Judging from the amount of times one hears statements like, 'Of course, Beethoven's metronome marks were all hopelessly fast', we can also assume that metronomes all ran at different speeds. To effect a compromise, the 'old guy with the white stick' was brought in. Known as 'the conductor' (as he had previously been working on the buses), he would stand at the front of the orchestra and languidly flap his stick in what was supposedly a rhythmic motion. This set an approximate tempo, but occasionally the old guy would remember how much alimony he was paying his four ex-wives, lose his temper, and speed up drastically in the middle of a slow passage.* Worse, the sudden onset of senility might cause the tempo to plummet to 5 b.p.m. This was clearly no good—something had to be done.

* *This condition, known as 'score rage', can strike without warning.*

John Travolta

After hundreds of years of tempo-related misery, the great break-through came in 1978 when it was discovered that the film actor John Travolta could walk at exactly 120 b.p.m. This caused great excitement in Hollywood, and as a result of this unique talent, Travolta was cast in the lead role in a number of screen musicals. To match his unwavering stride, all songs had to be written at 120 b.p.m., with the extra decree that each time one of Travolta's feet hit the ground, there should be a loud thump on a bass drum. The resulting style, called *disco,* became the soundtrack for the '80s . . . and the '90s . . . and the 2000s . . . and the '10s . . . and the '20s . . . .

Sorry, I was just having a bad dream there. Back in the real world, electronic metronomes now enable us to measure tempo precisely and consistently, and composers can specify tempos on their scores with some degree of confidence. The ubiquity of the click track may have had a mechanizing effect on contemporary music, but it has at least produced a generation of musicians who can play in metronomic time —no easy feat.

A Rough Guide to Tempo

At the end of the chapter you will find a tempo range chart, linked to some current pop music styles and the old Italian terms which have been in use since the 17th century. In those days, tempo measurement was a question of human, rather than mechanical calculation, so attempting to link a term like 'Allegro' to an exact b.p.m. figure may be an act of folly! The ephemeral nature of dance music will no doubt one day render jungle and drum'n'bass as redundant as the Twist and the Watusi, but I include them in the spirit of anthropological observation. These tempo ranges are only intended as the broadest of guides, and there will always be generic examples which fall outside the given limits.

Deciding a Tempo—Some Tips

Compositions often start with a simple drum beat, or a line played on a solo instrument. As you add instruments to the arrangement, you may find that your initial tempo has to be slowed to make space for the new sounds. This is especially true of songwriting, where the addition of a vocal line often requires a considerable adjustment to the speed of the backing track.

Even the most precise live musicians speed up into a chorus, or slow down in a quiet section. This helps the music to breathe, so if you are a composer working with an electronic click track, look for opportunities to subtly vary the tempo. This also applies to periods of silence; for example, a short pause following some dramatic event will work best if its tempo is slightly slower (1 or 2 b.p.m.) than the music surrounding it.

Human beings are not machines, and stage or studio nerves can push tempos through the roof, resulting in scrambled performances. Allow for this by taking a pocket metronome with you on stage, and counting in at a slightly slower speed (say, 4 b.p.m.) than normal. Over the course of the first 16 bars, the adrenalin factor will soon bring the song up to speed, but hopefully it will end up somewhere near its optimum tempo.

In some music, the tempo is best left to the performers' interpretation, while other pieces might benefit by indicating a range—say 130–140 b.p.m. Outside the rigidly controlled world of computer-driven music, there are too many variances of room acoustic, instrument sound and player ability for the idea of a 'perfect tempo' to have much meaning.

Tempo and Notational Style

Deciding on a tempo has a knock-on effect on how the music looks on paper. At the risk of annoying John Travolta, a 120 b.p.m. disco song could be written out at 60 b.p.m., with all the note durations halved—quarter notes would become 8th notes, 16th notes would sprout an extra tail and become 32nd notes, etc. This would alter the notational style of the music without affecting its real life speed. Alternatively, you could write the song out at 240 b.p.m., which would see quarter notes turned into half notes, etc. The first method would produce more note tails, the second more bar lines. The middle path, 120 b.p.m., conveys the musical message with as few symbols as possible, which should be the aim of all music notation.

Half and Double Time

You may occasionally see the instruction $\flat = \frac{1}{2}$ in a score. This is a way of indicating that the tempo has doubled—the new quarter note is the same length as the old 8th note! Examples of this somewhat brain-boggling system are shown below; in each case, the music to the right of the double bar line sounds identical to the music in the first bar.

A change to double or half time (as in the first four examples) could equally well be indicated by a new tempo marking, say, a leap from 80 to 160 b.p.m. or vice versa—this would require no change in the notational style. However, the 'x = y' system comes into its own when indicating a change from dotted to straight notes (or the other way round)—working out how to achieve the same effect with a tempo change instruction involves some rather tedious mathematics!

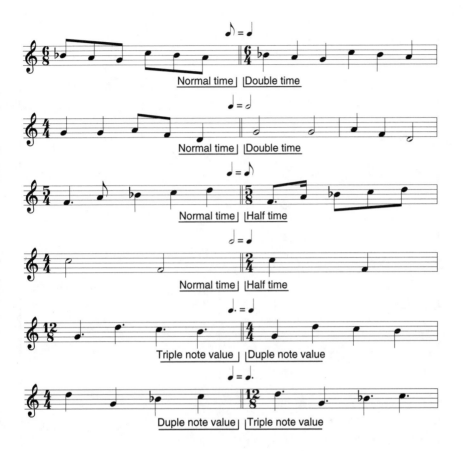

ROUGH TEMPO GUIDE

Pop Styles		Italian Terms* (Rough Approximations)	
Slow Ballad	♩ = 50 – 75	Largo	♩ = 40 – 60
Medium Ballad	♩ = 75 – 90	Lento	♩ = 50 – 66
Funk	♩ = 85 – 110	Larghetto	♩ = 60 – 66
Rock	♩ = 90 – 150	Adagio	♩ = 66 – 76
Disco	♩ = 120 – 130	Andante	♩ = 76 – 108
House	♩ = 124 – 135	Moderato	♩ = 108 – 120
Techno	♩ = 124 – 145		
Jungle	♩ = 150 – 200	Allegro**, Allegretto	♩ = 120 – 168
Drum'n'Bass	♩ = 150 – 200	Presto	♩ = 168 – 200
Speed Metal	♩ = 150 – 200		
Gong Kebyar***	♩ = 160 – 200+	Prestissimo	♩ = 200 – 200+

See Chapter Sixteen for translations of these, and other Italian terms.

*** The term 'Allegro' literally means 'cheerful', which in a musical context has come to mean fast, 'Allegretto' therefore meaning 'fairly fast'. In classical scores, these terms cover an even wider range of tempos than shown here.*

*** The breakneck gamelan style from Bali.*

T E N

Rhythm I

What Drummers Do

In the 1980s the charts were full of records with programmed
rhythm tracks, largely courtesy of Roger Linn's devilish Linndrum
device. Those recordings, considered ultra-modern at the time,
sound quaint now—the snare drums are way too loud, sometimes
obliterating the vocals, and the electronic toms (dew! dew! etc.) just
sound like a joke. Fortunately, we seem to have returned to an era of
comparative sonic realism where the drums you hear on records,
even if they were programmed, at least sound like the real thing.

Here's an admission: I played in rock bands from 1967 to 1980
without any real understanding of what drummers did. I knew that
they made plenty of noise, dictated the rhythmic agenda (or 'feel', as
we called it), and occasionally upped the tempo in alarming fashion
when they grew agitated or inebriated. I enjoyed playing with them
all immensely, but it was only when I started to program my own
rhythm tracks that I began to understand the complexities of what
these guys did. In this chapter, with the help of examples kindly
donated by drummers Gavin Harrison and Andy Duncan, I'll explain
some of the elements of rock drumming. Here's a key to the notated
sounds of the drum kit:

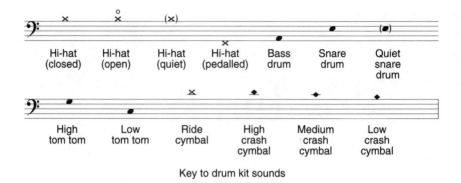

Key to drum kit sounds

Hi-Hat

The urgent tick of the closed hi-hat is rock music's accelerated heart-

beat: 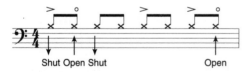 Even when unamplified, this

metallic sound will cut through virtually any din from the guitars!
The accents are most important, giving the rhythm its forward
momentum. Occasionally the hi-hat is played open (i.e., with the
pedal lifted), giving a splashy cymbal sound which is quickly shut
down on the next beat:

Shut Open Shut   Open

Bass and Snare Drums

Beats on the bass drum and snare drum are added to the hi-hat pulse
to create simple rock rhythms like:

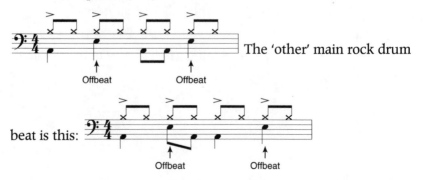

The 'other' main rock drum

Offbeat   Offbeat

beat is this:

Offbeat   Offbeat

(Note the slightly different bass drum pattern.) These two simple examples are probably the most common of all rock beats, and if you know how to play or program them, you are halfway to making a record! (Not a startlingly original one, but it's the thought that counts.)

As a rule of thumb, drummers usually mark the downbeat (first beat of the bar) with a bass drum, while adding snare drums on beats two and four—the off-beats. One exception is the famous '60s Tamla Motown snare on-beat:

Tamla Motown drum pattern

In moments of emotional crisis (or in disco music, where the bass drum plays on every quarter note beat) the drummer might play bass drum and snare together, but usually they are kept apart. The three elements of hi-hat, snare and bass drum thus represent the high, middle and low frequencies of the rock drum kit, and are its most important instruments.

Cymbals

In jazz, the ride cymbal is preferred as the main timekeeping instrument:

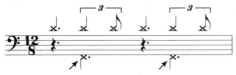

The classic 'ten-to-ten' jazz cymbal rhythm

With the ride marking time, the hi-hat is free to play the pedalled off-beats you see indicated. When played with the foot pedal, the hi-hat sounds quieter and less percussive than when hit with a stick, but it retains a clear, precise quality. Rock drummers also use the ride cymbal, but tend to omit the subtle embellishments of jazz drummers:

Crash cymbals are used to dramatically emphasize certain beats, often the first beat of a chorus or the final beat of a passage. Drummers like to make as much noise as possible, so will always add a bass drum or snare drum accent to a crash cymbal if they possibly can:

Any sane person would think one crash cymbal was enough, but rock drummers often have three or four to vary the sound of their mind-bendingly loud crashes:

(This presupposes, with sound levels rivalling that of an air raid, that anyone can hear the difference.) Though cymbals have no discernible fundamental pitch, their frequencies vary with size and thickness, so three different crash cymbals could be designated high, medium and low. Very small crash cymbals are called 'splash cymbals', and their high-pitched detonations are a welcome alternative to the overwhelming sonorities of the bigger cymbals.

Tom Toms

The tom toms are traditionally used for decorative patterns we call 'fills', for which the regular elements of the pulse are suspended. A drum fill often signals a change in the music, for example a fill into a song's chorus:

An 'intro fill' is often used at the beginning of a song, heralding the entry of the rest of the group:

Tamla Motown intro fill

Tom intro to Stewart/Gaskin arrangement of 'Subterranean Homesick Blues'

Sometimes the toms are used instead of the hi-hat or ride cymbal to

mark time:  . You can hear this excit-

ing rumble on the verses of the Rolling Stones' 'Brown Sugar'.

Syncopation

In the late '60s, James Brown and Sly & The Family Stone made groundbreaking records which pioneered the funk movement. Funk rhythms had their roots in the marching bands of New Orleans, and represented a breakaway from the rather foursquare drum rhythms of white pop. In the '50s, pop drummers would play 8th note rhythms

like:  at quick tempos. Slowing the

tempo a little gave musicians the chance to introduce 16th notes and play more complex syncopated patterns of this type:

16th note funk pattern

8th note funk pattern with snare syncopation

This effectively doubled the amount of rhythmic information and opened the floodgates for all manner of glorious syncopation. Pop music never looked back, but its highly developed rhythmic structure owes much to the visionary experiments of black musicians.

One facet of syncopation which rock musicians perform quite naturally is 'the push'. This involves anticipating the downbeat of a bar with an accent on the last 8th note of the previous bar:

If the downbeat is left silent (as in our example), this has the psychological effect of bringing it forward by half a beat. 16th note pushes are also quite common, especially in funk styles:

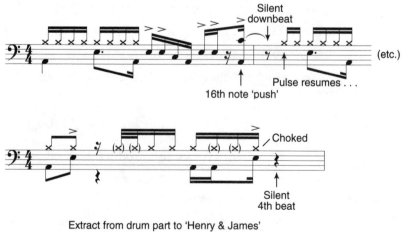

Extract from drum part to 'Henry & James'
(extended intro) by Stewart/Gaskin

Amongst novice musicians, there is a temptation to treat the accented beat as if it were the actual downbeat, which means that somewhere along the line, the music would have lost a 16th note! The way round this problem is to develop a strong inner sense of pulse, which clearly differentiates such syncopated offbeat accents from the main beat. Orchestral musicians seem to have a far harder time with this sort of thing than their rock counterparts. This is probably because Western classical music places much more store on notes and harmony than on rhythmic pulse, but one hopes this will balance out over the next twenty years or so. Viola players please note—all you have to do is listen to some James Brown records and tap your foot!

Balinese Drumming

The Western drum kit is a rather complicated industrial contraption, but exciting rhythms can be produced on a pair of simple hand drums, such as the Indian tabla. On the island of Bali, pairs of drum-mers play interlocking patterns on double-headed hand drums called *kendhang*. The right hand plays accents on one head of the drum, while the left hand fills in the non-accented beats on the other. Below is a typical drum pattern from Balinese processional music; as you can see, the first drummer's accents are echoed one 16th note later by the second drummer!

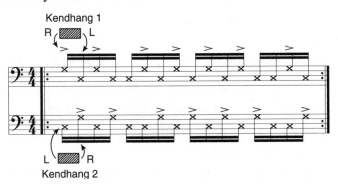

ELEVEN

Rhythm II

Metre and Time Signatures

For the sake of intelligibility and clarity of position, music is divided into bars, which are called 'measures' in the U.S.A. Without bar lines, we would be adrift in an ocean of notes and beats, but the vertical division of written music gives us a map, and a clear idea of where we are in terms of elapsed time.

Most music is written over some kind of regular pulse, and the organisation of that pulse into patterns of beats which can be represented visually is called *metre*. The metre of a piece of music is indicated by a time signature, which is shown at the beginning of a piece, and thereafter at any point where it changes. As you probably know, time signatures look like this: $\frac{3}{4}$ $\frac{12}{8}$ $\frac{2}{4}$ $\frac{5}{16}$ $\frac{3}{2}$ (etc.)

Irregular Time Signatures

A great deal of music (including practically all commercial pop) is written in 4/4, to the extent that some might think 4/4 is the only permissible metre. Of course, this is not the case. A friend of mine, Rick Biddulph, writes music which, quite unselfconsciously, turns out to contain bars of 5/4 and 7/4 within an overall 4/4 framework. His musical ideas develop organically, often guided by the rhythms of his lyrics, and the end result has a natural and characterful quality. Rick has some distant Greek ancestry, and Greek folk dances feature a profusion of 7/8, 9/8 and 13/8 metres which the dancers, despite possessing only the usual number of legs, have no difficulty negotiating. In the early '70s, English progressive rock groups (notably Soft Machine) played and composed effortlessly in all manner of irregular metres. Stravinsky's music contains passages where the time signature changes at every bar–if you can, check out the scores to his *Rite of Spring* or *Dumbarton Oaks* concerto. It would be inspiring to think that musical metres–and indeed, all elements of music–could be as varied and unpredictable as the forms and shapes of nature, but the forces of mechanization and commercialisation seem to stand in the way of that notion.

Having been force-fed a diet of 4/4 all our lives, it can be difficult at first to play in odd length metres like 7/8. One way to count this metre is to think of it as three whole beats plus one half beat; 9/8 would be 4 whole beats plus one half beat, and so on. The half beat can be felt as a kind of skip in a slower succession of beats. The advantage of this method is it reduces the amount of counting by 50%–trying to count all thirteen beats of a 13/8 bar is no fun, but subdividing it into six and a half longer beats gives you a chance to keep up with the pulse! Here is a table of odd metres divided in this fashion:

How to count irregular time signatures

You might also find it helpful, as I do, to think of bigger metres like 11/8 as a compound bar of 4/4 and 3/8.

In real terms, the half beat or skip may not occur at the end of the bar:

However, the maths still work out! When we first tackle irregular metres we all have to count hard, but with perseverance, they begin to feel as natural as 4/4.

Below are two examples of irregular time signatures played on drum kit and tuned percussion respectively. The first is a 13/8 pattern devised by Bill Bruford, which I've lifted from his 'Packet of 3' collection of sampled performances:

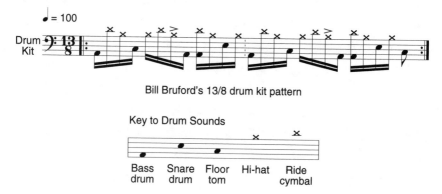

Bill Bruford's 13/8 drum kit pattern

Notice how the 13/8 is divided into two segments of 6/8 and 7/8; the latter is identical to the first, but with an extra floor tom beat added! The second example shows a repeated balafon (African xylophone) pattern from a tune called 'Ernest Scott Pursues a Theory' by Dirk Campbell:

Dirk Campbell's multi-metric balafon pattern

Dirk's rhythmic method is to alternate irregularly between groups of two and three beats, creating kaleidoscopic syncopations which one can never quite pin down. (The numbers underneath the lower stave indicate the beat groups.)

Odd-Numbered Note Groupings

You are no doubt familiar with the notational convention that a '3' written above or below a group of three notes means that they should be played in the space of two. Such groups are called 'triplets'. The concept extends to quintuplets (five notes played in the space of four) and duplets (two notes played in the space of three). Needless to say, composers like Frank Zappa have taken the idea to extremes by dividing quarter notes into eleven, and so on. (Study the score to Zappa's 'The Black Page' for the full, terrifying story.)

Personally, I experience enough trouble playing one note in the space of one, but here is a short table of rhythmic note groupings for your edification:

Rhythmic note groupings from 1 to 10

As an exercise, play repeatedly through the first eight against a metronome click of 45 b.p.m.—the five- and seven-groups will probably require the most practise! When you've done with that, try the groupings below:

Duplets and quadruplets

These duplet and quadruplet groups—respectively, two and four notes played in the space of three—may also be notated as dotted notes (shown in brackets).

Sometimes, especially when transcribing solos, it is convenient to decide, for example, that a musician has played seven notes in the space of four:

The reality is that the player (probably a jazz musician) has executed a quick burst of ascending notes at the fastest speed his fingers will allow, and seven of these fast notes happen to last about one beat. If a whole ensemble were to repeat such a rhythm for a few beats, the listener's impression would be that the music had changed tempo!

Polyrhythms and Rhythmic Cycles

What happens if we play in two time signatures simultaneously? We get fired by our record company, but that's not the whole story. Interesting and unusual rhythmic textures can be produced by overlaying a repeated rhythmic pattern over another of a different metre. The patterns may be of any length you choose, but they must share the same basic pulse and be played at the same tempo!

To illustrate this musical idea, here are two patterns of different length:

The first is seven beats long, the second only five beats long. Obviously, if we play them together at the same tempo, the 5/4 pattern

will finish before the 7/4. However, to keep the ball rolling, we simply repeat the 5/4. When the 7/4 pattern finishes, we repeat that, without dropping a beat . . . the two patterns thus repeat indefinitely, their start points getting more and more out of sync, but held together by their common quarter note pulse.

To hear how this sounds, you need either two musicians (preferably of the patient and willing variety—avoid heavy rock bass players) or a MIDI sequencer. The music's main effect is to obliterate the bar line with a nebulous swirl of notes, but despite the feeling of dislocation, the ever-changing, shifting rhythmic textures produced are quite delightful. The overall pattern is not entirely unpredictable: after the 7/4 pattern has played five times and the 5/4 pattern seven times, we arrive back at the beginning, having completed one rhythmic cycle. Such rhythmic exercises, where different metres are superimposed, are called *polyrhythms*.

I'll leave you with two more examples of polyrhythms which you may like to try out on a rainy day. The first is a combination of two double-handed keyboard patterns, one in 12/8, the other in 11/8. Both use the right hand to play off-beats in between the left hand's beats, but the 11/8 skips an offbeat as it returns to the beginning.

The overlapping note ranges require careful hand positioning—try placing the right thumb over the left! If you are playing these parts on a keyboard or workstation with sampled instrument sounds, a soft marimba program with a little release decay* will work well.

*Keyboard programmer's term for the portion of a sound which, after the fingers have been lifted, sustains for a short while, then dies away.

My final polyrhythm is one of the first pieces of music I ever wrote. These are two keyboard patterns, the first (in 17/8) with a chiming quality, the second (in 11/8) a slightly jazzy riff with a see-sawing bass line. (The latter may be played by guitar and bass if any band is brave enough to try it!) As you will have worked out by now, a full cycle is completed when the first pattern has been played eleven times and the second seventeen times. That gives plenty of opportunity for things to go wrong, but while gritting your teeth during the fourteenth reiteration of the 11/8 riff, console yourself with the thought that by the end of the cycle, every possible vertical juxtaposition of the two patterns' notes will have sounded.

T W E L V E

Computers & MIDI

The extent to which music-making has become bound up with the computer industry can be measured by the ever-growing number of periodicals which exist primarily to review music software. Once an amusing diversion, these products now dominate the music scene. Young musicians, rather than form a band, prefer to work in their bedrooms with soundcards and sequencing software. The classical composer, though perhaps all at sea with the idea of MIDI, buys expensive scoring software, and an even more expensive, dedicated computer on which to run it. The studio boss, keen to cut costs while offering superficially impressive technical specs, junks his old multi-track tape recorder and arranges finance on a hard disk system which integrates digital multitrack recording with a sophisticated MIDI sequencing program.

Where will it all end? It won't. Whether we like it or not, these products now have to be seen as bona fide musical tools, and in this chapter we'll look at how computers and MIDI handle the intricacies of musical performance, real or virtual.

How MIDI Works

MIDI stands for 'Musical Instrument Digital Interface', and was pioneered in the early '80s by Dave Smith, American inventor of the Prophet synthesizer. (Aptly named—it was a very good instrument in its time.) Dave's idea, at first viewed with suspicion by some other manufacturers, transformed the musical industry by providing a common language for electronic musical equipment.

The digital code devised by Dave Smith and other manufacturers was in essence quite simple. (If I can understand it, it must be.) It boils down to this: when you press a key on a MIDI keyboard, a burst of digital data is generated, which incorporates the following information:

A **MIDI channel** number,

a **note-on** code

and a **velocity value**.

When the key is released, a further **note-off** code is generated.

MIDI Parameters

The MIDI spec allows for 128 possible notes, and the diagram at the end of the chapter shows the MIDI note numbering system for a standard five-octave keyboard. The player has a choice of 16 MIDI channels, selected at the master keyboard by setting a 'transmit channel' number from 1 to 16. This creates the possibility of the 'MIDI orchestra'—16 MIDI devices, each with its own instrument sound, all controlled from the same source! Early MIDI synthesizers were designed to respond to only one MIDI channel at a time, but contemporary models offer multi-channel 'multitimbral' facilities in which up to 16 different sounds can play independently.

The 'velocity value' of a note is determined by an internal sensor, which measures the speed of a key's depression. The velocity of the note is electronically linked to its output volume, giving a dynamic response akin to that of an acoustic instrument—the harder (and therefore faster) the player strikes the key, the louder the signal that emerges. This enables the subtle dynamic nuances of performance to be encoded as MIDI data.

In addition to the basic note, velocity and channel numbers, MIDI offers elaborate 'controller' information such as keyboard aftertouch, pitch bend, pitch and panning modulation, sustain pedal, etc. These can all be generated by the player as part of a live performance, and although this adds up to a considerable amount of data, it happily passes down one MIDI cable and arrives at the other end more or less instantaneously! I say 'more or less' because the processing time of some receiving MIDI devices can cause small timing delays when large amounts of data have to be decoded.

Sequencers and Computers

Before long, someone realized that MIDI data could be recorded and played back in real time. (Though not as an audio signal—the bandwidth of MIDI is too high to be reproduced by conventional tape recorders.) As a result, the eerie spectacle of an unmanned keyboard confidently blasting out its absent owner's performance swiftly became commonplace. The creative potential was enormous, and even early sequencers like the Roland MSQ700 offered eight record tracks which could be used to create MIDI compositions for up to 16 independent instruments. Later sequencers offered extensive editing facilities, so wrong notes could be corrected or erased, and missing notes reinstated. Performances you could edit? Music with *no musicians*? The recording industry could hardly believe its luck.

It was only a matter of time before companies began manufacturing software programs that duplicated and extended sequencers' MIDI capabilities. In the 1980s, the Atari computer, hooked up to a MIDI keyboard and rack-mount sampler, became a standard item of musician's kit. Although several excellent hardware-based sequencers are still manufactured, computers have now largely taken over as the standard MIDI recording device.

The Click Track

In order to make musical sense of the crazed nonsense which appears at their MIDI in sockets, computers relate the stream of MIDI data to an internal clock, which has an electronic metronome attached. The metronome's tempo defaults to 120 b.p.m., but that may be altered. (Though don't breathe a word to John Travolta.) The idea is that the musician should listen to the click of the electronic metronome and play along *in time*, which is actually a very tall order—it takes years to get used to playing with this nasty little noise, and most musicians (myself included) tend to part company with it after a while. At first, you will swear blind that the click is slowing down, but the sad reality is *you are speeding up*—or vice versa.

Clock Pulses

To deceive the eye, motion pictures flash by at 24 frames per second, and to deceive the ear, computers divide time into even smaller slices called (in at least one manufacturer's terminology) *clock pulses.* A clock pulse is a tiny subdivision of a quarter note, and the number of clock pulses per quarter note is often abbreviated to 'p.p.q.' (pulses per quarter note). The p.p.q. value of a MIDI system is known as its 'timing resolution'. 96 p.p.q. is the minimum standard nowadays, but some systems go as high as 960 p.p.q.!

So, you howl, how long is a bloody clock pulse? That depends on the tempo of the music. At the default tempo of 120 b.p.m., a clock pulse in a 96 p.p.q. system would be just over 5 milliseconds long. At 200 b.p.m., it would be a little over 3 milliseconds. In a system offering 960 p.p.q., one clock pulse would last only half a millisecond at 120 b.p.m.. The ear cannot hear the difference between two events half a millisecond apart, so this timing resolution should do us nicely for the time being.

(The relationship of note values to clock pulses is shown in a diagram at the end of the chapter.)

Quantization

Most people want to record music in 4/4 time, so computers use that as their default time signature. (This can be changed by the user at any point.) During a MIDI recording, the computer records every single musical event, including note-ons, note-offs and *controller information* such as pitch bends and sustain pedal actions. Every piece of information is logged precisely with a clock pulse number, and its position within each nominal 4/4 bar is noted. This great string of events is stored in the computer's memory as a *sequence*.

In terms of clock pulses, it is unlikely that your MIDI performance will be 100% rhythmically accurate, and even if it were, it would probably sound rather stiff and mechanical. This is OK—although some are able to keep pace with a click, human beings do not play exactly in time; the likelihood is that some notes will be late, while others will be early. Using a matrix of 96 p.p.q., a typical performance of four quarter notes within a bar might look something like this:

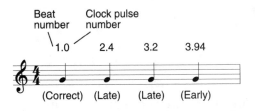

If you wish, you can use the computer's editing facilities to automatically correct these small timing erroneities. This technique is called *quantization*, and it is done by telling the machine to correct notes' positions to the nearest quarter note, 8th note, or whatever. Deciding the quantize setting can be a difficult decision when different note values co-exist within the same bar (which they almost always do), but as a rule of thumb, always quantize to the smallest note value your performance uses—in my experience, this is very often a 16th note.

After quantization, the display for the corrected performance would read as follows:

However, I would not advise this 'hard quantization' for anything other than click tracks and basic rhythm parts, as it sounds too stiff when applied to the whole track. A subtler approach, 'soft quantize' or 'percentage quantize', lets you move all notes back a given percentage (say, 60%) of the way towards their correct positions. This gives a less rigid effect, but personally, I avoid such drastic global approaches when editing my own performances. Although it takes longer, I tend to go through the MIDI data just tidying up the odd misplaced note, as this seems a better way to preserve the spirit of the performance.

Despite the ultimate editing control offered by computers, it's much better to learn to play your parts in time with no mistakes (that's what you have to do when you play live, after all) than spending hours using the computer to tidy up a sloppy performance!

Computer Pitfalls

I could fill a book with this one, but here's a small but annoying problem: if you play a downbeat of a bar a fraction early, the computer will log that event as falling in the previous bar. Any editing work on that bar (say, an increase in MIDI velocity/volume) will now affect your early downbeat, which is probably not what you had in mind musically.

When programming rhythm tracks for a friend's album, he asked for my help with a knotty sequencing problem—'I've wiped this bar completely', he said, 'but I still keep hearing a long bass note all the way through it.' Looking at the computer display confirmed there was no MIDI data in the bar, but some bars previously, there had been a MIDI 'sustain pedal on' command. The corresponding 'sustain pedal off' command had been erased, so as far as the computer was concerned, the sustain pedal was down, and staying that way till someone instructed otherwise. The problem was easily solved by inserting a 'sustain pedal off' command, but details like this illustrate how literal-minded and niggly computers can be—and that's on the days when they don't crash!

MIDI note numbers on a standard 5-octave keyboard

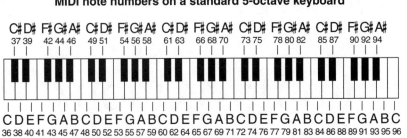

(MIDI notes outside the 36–96 range may be generated on a
5-octave keyboard by using its 'key transpose' function.)

		Fraction	No. of clock pulses				
		of bar	96 ppq	192 ppq	384 ppq	480 ppq	960 ppq
𝅝	(whole note)	= whole	384	768	1536	1920	3840
𝅗𝅥	(half note)	= half	192	384	768	960	1920
𝅗𝅥³	(half note triplet)	= third	128	256	512	640	1280
𝅘𝅥	(quarter note)	**= quarter**	**96**	**192**	**384**	**480**	**960**
𝅘𝅥³	(quarter note triplet)	= sixth	64	128	256	320	640
𝅘𝅥𝅮	(1/8th note)	= eighth	48	96	192	240	480
𝅘𝅥𝅮³	(1/8th note triplet)	= 1/12th	32	64	128	160	320
𝅘𝅥𝅯	(1/16th note)	= 1/16th	24	48	96	120	240
𝅘𝅥𝅯³	(1/16th note triplet)	= 1/24th	16	32	64	80	160
𝅘𝅥𝅰	(1/32nd note)	= 1/32nd	12	24	48	60	120
𝅘𝅥𝅰³	(1/32nd note triplet)	= 1/48th	8	16	32	40	80
𝅘𝅥𝅱	(1/64th note)	= 1/64th	6	12	24	30	60
𝅘𝅥𝅱³	(1/64th note triplet)	= 1/96th	4	8	16	20	40

The relationship of note values to clock pulses in 96, 192, 384, 480 and 960 ppq systems

THIRTEEN

Improvisation/ Composition I

Improvisation

Improvisation is composing done in real time. That makes it sound hard, but actually anyone can do it—all you have to do is learn how to play a few notes on an instrument, and then make something up. If no instrument is available, you can just sing something instead, like my next door neighbour Cecil who makes up little songs for his grandchildren. The important thing is to enjoy doing it, and not worry about whether it is 'good' or not.

Worrying about whether music is 'good' is a really efficient way to kill it, because in one step it transforms the fun of music-making into doubts and fears. Once the nagging doubt—'I enjoyed playing that, but was it any *good*?'—takes hold, it can put people off music for life. Parents sometimes unwittingly aid this process by insisting that their children stop messing about on their instruments and play some 'proper' music instead. Why spoil the kids' fun? All music is proper if it enriches the spirit. While on this subject, here's another suggestion: we should encourage music students to invent things, not just to be human jukeboxes who reproduce the compositions of others at the push of a button. To me, there are few sadder musical spectacles than the concert pianist who has studied eight hours a day for twenty years to tackle the dizzy intricacies of Rachmaninov, but lacks the confidence to play a single note of original music.

Making a Start

Fine words indeed, but how do you improvise? The way I do it is simple: take three or four notes and mess around with their rhythm. For example, I might choose these four notes:

—and then, by experimenting with different rhythms and note orders, end up with a pattern like:

I might then go on to add some chords:

or just use the right hand phrase on its own as a rhythm pattern. Another approach is to play sustained bass notes in the left hand, and make up some rhythms in the right:

After a while, ideas will start to coalesce, and I might find myself repeating and fixing things . . . as soon as you do that, improvisation has given way to the more considered process of composition. Nothing wrong with that, but in order to generate the maximum number of musical ideas in a short time, I find it best to keep my improvisation fairly free. Often, I just ramble on, or if I find something I like, I repeat it over and over, which helps me remember it later. All this probably sounds pretty aimless to anyone walking past my music room door, but as long as I'm enjoying myself, I know that some usable ideas will come. The main thing is to avoid making decisions or value judgements too early on, so that the music has a chance to emerge from whatever mysterious crevice of the human soul it hides in!

Composition I

Dan Quayle (the rather stupid American ex-vice-president) once said that space was 'a big area'. So is composition, and writing about it in one or two chapters is a bit like looking at the sky through a keyhole . . . nevertheless, I offer the following suggestions in the hope of inspiring some of you to start exploring those stellar reaches.

Composing with Melodies

All composers need limitations. Imagine all the notes of the piano— there are an awful lot of them, and if you had to use every single one in a tune, you'd be in big trouble. To get started, and to combat the 'blank sheet' syndrome which affects every composer at some stage, it is sometimes useful (as in the improvising example above) to take a small selection of notes and use them to form melodies.

A good place to start is the pentatonic scale, which is formed by adding an E flat to the four notes used earlier:

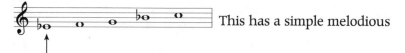 This has a simple melodious

sound, which can be exploited to write tunes like:

 A melodic phrase like this

could be balanced by an answering phrase:

Notice how the rhythm of the second phrase contrasts with the first.

A melody's rhythm is as important as its notes, and notes may have to be left out, added or relocated to make the rhythm work. The following example shows our two-bar melody with a new rhythm and a few added (arrowed) notes:

Once you have settled on a tune, you could add a bass line, or even a second melody line with an independent rhythm. The latter style of writing, little used in commercial music nowadays, is called counterpoint. Here is a full version of our original melody (slightly amended at the very end) with a bass line and two contrapuntal melody lines:

The addition of the notes of D and A (arrowed) to the original scale means we are now using a type of C minor scale:

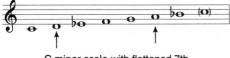

C minor scale with flattened 7th

Now you have a four-part arrangement (albeit a short one), it is fun to orchestrate the lines. I worked out these parts using four instrument sounds: (from the top) Fender Rhodes, trumpet, brass section and fretless bass, all of which you would commonly find in a keyboard workstation. The addition of extra lines (especially the bass line) has chordal implications, but let's stick with the concept of single line composition for the moment.

You can vary the flavour of your melodic lines simply by changing the scale. The 'Lydian' scale (a favourite of mine, named after the old white-note mode based on F to F) has a more mystical-sounding effect:

If major and minor scales sound too safe, you can get weirder by using the slightly mad 'alternating tone and semitone' scale based on C#:

This line would sound effective on an oboe or clarinet. But if you want to make an original and forthright musical statement with pronounced anti-social overtones, take the plunge and scare your neighbours with something like:

. This atonal riff could be

hammered out by unison distorted guitar and bass, pounded on the low end of a piano, or taken up three octaves and bashed out on a xylophone. Whatever the presentation or orchestration, the choice of notes, angular phrasing and metre would make it sound scary!

(Other scales and modes may be found in Chapter Three.)

Composing with Chords

Having enjoyed your rendition of the last example played at 300 watts, the neighbours are probably now dialling the police, so as we await the approaching wail of sirens, let's talk about chordal composition. This is my favourite musical method, though there are many others which work. Partly as an exercise and partly as compositional strategy, I often pick a chord whose sound I like and play it in different keys:

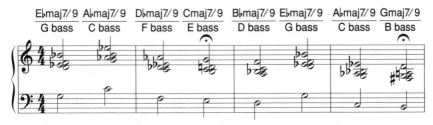

These experiments have been known to generate mistakes when my fingers pick out the wrong intervals, but sometimes the 'wrong' chords sound good too! Whether it occurs by accident or design, I'm happy to use whatever I find.

The idea of chord sequences needs no explanation, but one fruitful trick is to repeat a sequence in a new key. If I can find a key relationship where the new key leads me back naturally to the first, so much the better, but sometimes I have to keep changing key until I find a way home! Here's an example of a completely circular sequence, which, by moving down a major 3rd three times, eventually arrives back where it started:

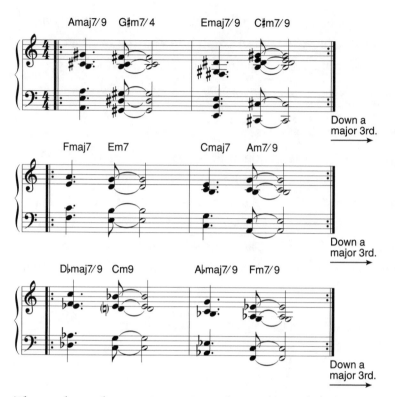

(Play each two-bar section twice or four times.) This seemingly end-less modulation produces a feeling of 'lost in harmony', which I find very enjoyable.

Chords can be given a unity of sound by using a common top note:

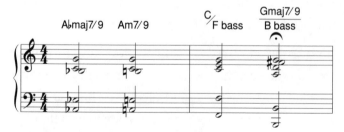

In the '70s, one of my main compositional techniques was to assemble sequences of chords whose top notes could be arranged and extended to form melodies:

The melody line was then extracted and given to a guitar or a vocal, while I played the full version on keyboard.

Most songs are written over 'block chords'—that is, the notes of the chords all sound together, and everybody plays the chord changes at the same time, usually at the top of a bar. A nice way of breaking up this monotony is to play the notes of the chord in *arpeggio* form:

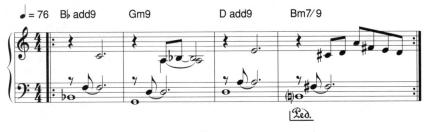

Extract from '*As Far As Dreams Can Go*'

(A simplified version of this sequence appeared in Chapter Two.) If you can get your fingers round them in time, *passing chords* are also a useful way of breaking up the otherwise stolid plod of chord changes. The following example shows the simple four-chord sequence from the chorus of 'New Jerusalem' (also seen in Chapter Two) as it really sounds, with passing chords (arrowed) inserted between the main changes:

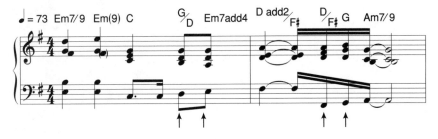

As we saw with the contrapuntal music earlier in this chapter, temporary chords are formed when melody lines overlap. These could be seen as an incidental byproduct of melodic development, or as the main point of the exercise! No one handled the balancing of melodic and harmonic development in counterpoint better than J. S. Bach, and I would encourage every musician, whether pop or classical, to study his work carefully.

FOURTEEN

Composition II

Composing with Rhythm

For a while, forget about notes. (If that's possible in a book which keeps screaming about them.) You can write superb music with no pitches at all, by combining percussion sounds with complementary rhythm patterns. In Chapter Ten we saw a pair of interlocking drum beats from Balinese *Beleganjur* ceremonial music, whose function is to scare off demons. To this end, the music is played on drums, gongs and small pairs of hand cymbals called *ceng ceng*, all of which make a huge amount of din. Here is an example of what the *ceng ceng* play:

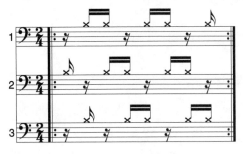

Balinese *ceng ceng* patterns

As you can see, these interlocking patterns are based on a rhythm which is successively displaced by one 16th note beat from player to player, and this simple but brilliant idea produces a scintillating (though deafening) rhythmic racket. Western musicians could play similar patterns on wood blocks, claves or cowbells, though there is always a risk of the audience running away along with the demons.

African drum music is the holy grail of interlocking rhythms, and sometimes these interlocking patterns are played on cowbells. There are many types of bell, from the tiny *frikiwa* (a sort of metal castanet, played with a metal thumb ring) to the large *gankogwe* (double iron bells mounted on a single stem, ancestors of the Latin American *agogo* bells). The larger of the two *gankogwe* bells produces a pure low tone, while its smaller companion produces a seemingly random pitch between a 5th and an octave higher. (As long as there is some marked variation of tuning from low bell to high bell, it seems the exact pitches are not important.) The following shows examples of typical patterns–they could be played on four sets of *gankogwe* or *agogo* bells, or on unpitched cowbells like the *atokwe*, a banana-shaped slit cowbell. In the latter case, the lower note should be played as an open, ringing hit and the upper note a muted stroke:

African cowbell patterns

To these cowbell patterns, we can add a different set of interlocking African drum rhythms:

African drum patterns

The first and second patterns should be played on small to medium hand drums, with the lower pitch signifying an open tone, and the upper a muted hit. The third line works well on *dondon* or talking drum, whose pitch the player can vary greatly (and thereby articulate speech-like messages) by squeezing the drum's tension strings between arm and body. The fourth line is a part I invented, which should be played on some deep-toned drum–if nothing else were available, a rock bass drum would do. Adding these parts to the cow-bell patterns throws the rhythmic feel into delightful confusion. For the most part, the cowbell patterns have a 6/4, quarter note flavour, but the drum parts emphasize the dotted quarter note, 3+3+3+3 beat feel. This sort of ambiguity is a delight, and the diversity and power of African rhythms are comparable in standing to the harmonic achievements of Western music.

If no acoustic percussion instruments are available to you, sampled drum and percussion sounds are the next best thing (and will be a lot more popular with your long-suffering neighbours). With a little skill-ful programming, Latin American percussion sounds such as shakers, claves, congas, bongos and cowbells can be combined with drum kit sounds into very effective rhythm tracks, as shown in this example:

Latin American percussion + drum kit

If you swap this now standard percussion menu for the more exotic sounds of Japanese or Middle Eastern hand drums, Indonesian gamelan or Thai gong-chimes, you can compose interesting and original-sounding music for virtual percussion orchestras of your own invention.

The large memory capacity of samplers now means that very convincing dynamics (for example, incremental velocity cross-switching between successively louder drum strokes) can be built into the programming of sampled sounds, creating tracks which sound virtually indistinguishable from live performances. This becomes literally so when real performance samples (often called *loops*) are added to the mix–these short slices of rhythmic musical activity, often two or four bars in length, are convincing until one becomes aware of their constant repetition!

Composing with Sound

(Bassoonists can skip this section if they wish.) One of the greatest moments I ever experienced in music was when, playing a sample of a skylark down at quarter speed, I realized the damn thing was singing in a precise, complex language not unlike morse code. This insight into the wonders of nature was made possible by a cheap but highly effective Casio FZ1 sampler, which I still own. If you are into high-fidelity audiophile sounds, employing the extreme transposition facility of this machine is probably not a good idea . . . but if you want to hear a grainy, raucous, metallic, barely recognizable version of the original sample that sounds as though it is being played back though the speakers of a Venusian ice cream van, then the Casio's the gadget for you.

By the simple technique of playing back samples at the wrong speed, I have created sounds like the Kraken waking (female vocalist speaking Indonesian phrases, slowed down four octaves), an 'I speak

your weight' machine colliding with an asteroid (eight identical samples of a TV game show presenter yelling over some background
sound effect, all played back on the same key with 12-semitone pitch
bends), and other noises too weird to describe. Sampling bits of unre-
lated sound from the television is also a source of endless fun, as char-
acters often shout things like 'You've gone too far this time, Susan!'
which can be spun into a track just after the guitar solo. Currently, I
am looking forward to working a long, rambling, barely comprehen-
sible answerphone message from a Japanese acquaintance into a
recording. Quite how much of this the ear could stand in undiluted
form is debatable, but in conjunction with smoother keyboard sounds
playing conventional parts, samplers can add a welcome hint of the
irrational. I'm sure the early *musique concrète* composers like Varèse
would have enjoyed this surreal ability to play around with sound.

Unpitched or Pitched Sounds?

By some insane quirk of psychology, a sampler can turn an
unpitched sound into a pitched one. A dropped metal weight may
seem to have no definite pitch, but once it has been sampled and
played back at different pitches on a keyboard, the fundamental note
of the sound becomes much more apparent:

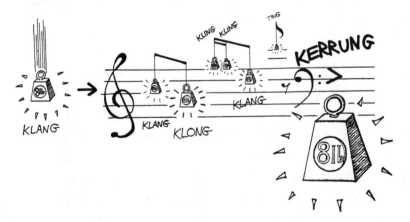

How a sampler transforms unpitched sound into pitched sound

FIFTEEN

Pitch Ranges & Transpositions

The following summary of instruments' pitch ranges also appeared at the end of my first book, but I make no apology for including it again (with some additions)—it is the section I personally find most useful, and I want to make sure it stays in print! Its purpose is not merely to haughtily inform you of a contrabassoon's bottom note or a piccolo's top one, but also to encourage you to orchestrate your music with instruments outside the conventional rock armoury of guitar, keyboards, bass, drums and the occasional squealing saxophone. If you should suddenly 'hear' an oboe part for one of your tunes, you can avoid making impossible demands on the player by checking the oboe's range here before you write its melody. (It should also go without saying that a real oboe, unlike a sampled one, can only play one note at a time!)

Vocal Ranges

Before launching into the list of instruments, we should take a careful look at something more fundamental: vocal ranges. These are commonly misunderstood—not everyone realises, for example, that singers have widely different vocal ranges, or even that women and men tend to sing in different registers! One story illustrates the problems that this can cause. A friend spent months of studio time recording his solo album. Having completed the backing tracks, he asked my partner Barbara Gaskin to sing one of the songs, assuring her that 'the tune should be OK for you, because I can sing it!' The tune, which spanned an unusually wide range, turned out to be in completely the wrong key for Barbara. In one register, the low notes were fine, but the high notes were up in 'Bee Gees on helium' range. Transposing the whole thing down an octave brought the high notes into a manageable register, but pushed the low notes down into sub-sonic Lee Marvin 'Wandering Star' territory. There were only two solutions to this predicament: either completely re-write the vocal tune, or re-record the backing track in a new key, six semitones lower. In the end we decided on the latter, which took two days of studio time and a lot of sweat recreating the sounds. Had all this been conducted outside the cosy world of home studios, it would have been a very costly mistake.

A quick perusal of the following chart of vocal ranges should ensure you never fall into the same trap—if this saves you money, be sure to send me a percentage!

Vocal Ranges

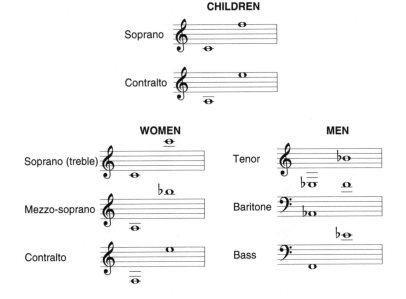

Singers may not be at their most expressive when straining for their highest or lowest notes, so you should try to pitch your vocal melodies somewhere comfortably in the middle of the singer's range. Low notes can be very effective, but they tend to sound breathier and quieter than high notes. Wherever possible, play through your arrangement with the singer to identify any problem areas. You may find that changing key by as little as a semitone makes a noticeable difference to the vocal performance, so be prepared to lean your song's backing in a new key!

Instrument Ranges

Much the same goes for instruments, although they are not quite so sensitive to slight changes of register. The ranges given are for general purposes, but the upper extremities will vary from player to player. In some cases (for example, trumpet) higher notes than those shown can be produced, but their musical quality cannot be guaranteed! If in doubt, check your melody's highest and lowest notes with the instrumentalist you have in mind.

Instrument ranges and transpositions

(Transposing instruments are marked *)

Instrument	Range *(written)* Sounds	Parts written	Clef commonly used

Instrument	Parts written	Clef commonly used
*Guitar	Up an octave	Treble
*Bass Guitar	Up an octave	Bass
Acoustic piano	Same	Two linked staves, treble and bass
*Sopranino Sax (E flat)	Down a minor 3rd	Treble
*Soprano Sax (B flat)	Up a tone	Treble
*Alto Sax (E flat)	Up a major 6th	Treble
*Tenor Sax (B flat)	Up an octave and a tone	Treble
*Baritone Sax (E flat)	Up an octave and a major 6th	Treble
*Bass Sax (B flat)	Up 2 octaves and a tone	Treble
*Trumpet & Cornet (B flat)	Up a tone	Treble
*Flugelhorn	Up a tone	Treble
Trombone	Same	Treble and bass (jazz), alto and tenor (orchestra)
Bass trombone	Same	Treble and bass (jazz), alto and tenor (orchestra)
Tuba (B flat)	Same	Bass
*French Horn (F)	Up a perfect 5th	Treble and bass

SAXOPHONES

BRASS

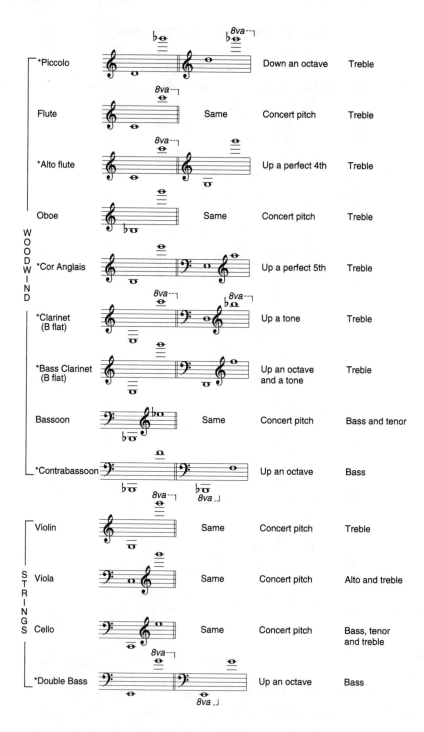

Instrument	Range *(written)*	Sounds	Parts written	Clef commonly used
*Celeste			Down an octave	Treble
*Glockenspiel			Down 2 octaves	Treble
*Xylophone			Down an octave	Treble
Marimba		Same	Concert pitch	Bass and treble
Bass Marimba		Same	Concert pitch	Bass and treble
Vibraphone		Same	Concert pitch	Treble
Tubular Bells		Same	Concert pitch	Treble
Timpani		Same	Concert pitch	Bass
Harp		Same	Concert pitch	Two linked staves, treble and bass
Harpsichord		Same	Concert pitch	Two linked staves, treble and bass
*Chapman Stick (10 string)			Up an octave	Treble and bass

The instrument column also shows the bracketed label **TUNED PERC** spanning Xylophone through Timpani.

(I should once again remind you that transposing instruments, for reasons too tedious to go into here, produce notes at a different pitch from those indicated on paper. I tend to agree with John Lennon's view of this—'That's stupid!')

SIXTEEN

Symbols & Expressions

Music has a large vocabulary (too large, I sometimes think) of signs, symbols and terms. It would take an entire dictionary to list them all, but I've compiled a few of the most common and useful here. The widespread use of Italian words reflects that country's former position as centre of the European musical world; however, non-Italian composers should feel free to use their native tongue, indicating 'lively' or *'aufgeweckt'* rather than *'vivace'*! Despite the waning of Italian influence, it is likely that simple terms like *'forte'* and *'piano'* (loud and soft) will remain in universal use.

1. Symbols

Pitch

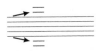

Stave

Ledger lines

Treble (G) clef

Bass (F) clef

Alto or tenor (C) clef

Middle C (treble clef)

Middle C (bass clef)

Middle C (alto clef)

Middle C (tenor clef)

♯

Sharp

♭

Flat

𝄪

Double sharp

♭♭

Double flat

♮

Natural

Key signature

8 ⌐----------⌐

Up an octave

8 ------------⌡

Down an octave

Written   Sounds

Grace note or *acciaccatura*

Trill

Rhythm and Tempo

Note   Rest

Double whole note (breve)

Whole note (semibreve)

Half note (minim)

Quarter note (crotchet)

8th note (quaver)

16th note (semiquaver)

32nd note (demisemiquaver)

64th note (hemidemisemiquaver)

Dotted half note. Dots add 50% to a note's value.

Dotted quarter note (etc.) Double dots may also be used, adding 75% to a note's value.

Tie (attaches notes of the same pitch to create longer rhythmic values)

Duplet

Triplet

Quintuplet (etc., see Chapter Eleven)

Abbreviation for fast repeated notes

♩ = 100

Tempo of 100 quarter note beats per minute

Metre and Repeat Signs

Bar line

Double bar line (used at end of
piece, or end of section)

One bar's rest (whole note rest is
used, irrespective of time signature)

Eight bars' rest

Time signature

C

Common time (abbreviation for 4/4)

¢

Alla breve (abbreviation for 2/2)

Repeat

Repeat with different endings

Repeat previous bar

Repeat previous two bars

⊕ Coda

Coda - Final passage

𝄋

Segno - Sign

D.S. al Coda

Dal Segno al Coda - Play as far as the sign,
then go straight to the ending

D.C.

Dal Capo - Play from the beginning

Rhythmic Expression

Accent

Staccato - detached, short

Staccatissimo - very short

Tenuto - play full length

Sforzando - forcibly accented

Slur - play smoothly (see also 'legato')

Phrase mark - placed over a group of notes, indicates that those notes should be articulated as one phrase

Pause sign

Dynamics

Crescendo - growing louder

Diminuendo (*decrescendo*) - growing quieter

fff	*Molto Fortissimo*	Extremely loud
ff	*Fortissimo*	Very loud
f	*Forte*	Loud
mf	*Mezzo forte*	Fairly loud
mp	*Mezzo piano*	Fairly quiet
p	*Piano*	Quiet
pp	*Pianissimo*	Very quiet
ppp	*Molto Pianissimo*	Extremely quiet
sf, sfz	*Sforzando*	Forcibly
sfp	*Sforzando-piano*	Play quietly immediately after accent
rf	*Rinforzando*	A sudden increase in volume

Performance Techniques

Arpeggio

Tremolo, Tremolando - Repeat note (or notes) as fast as possible, not necessarily in time

French Horn: Stopped (hand inserted in bell)

Strings: Up bow

Strings: Down bow

Strings: Natural harmonic (produces note one octave higher)

Strings: Artificial harmonic (written 4th above note—produces note two octaves higher)

Piano: Sustain pedal depressed

Piano: Sustain pedal lifted

2. Expressions (Mainly Italian)

Short Words

A	At, to, by
Col, colla, con	With
Da, Dal	From
Mene	Less
Molto	Much
Piu	More
Poco	A little
Sempre	Always
Senza	Without
Sotto	Below
Sul	On
- ma non troppo	But not too much!

Playing Styles

Piano

Tre corde	'Three strings' – Lift piano soft pedal
Una corda	'One string' – Depress piano soft pedal

Strings

Arco	Played with bow
Pizzicato	Plucked with fingers
Detaché	Detached, each note sounding separately (opposite of *Legato*)
Spiccato	With bow leaping from the strings between detached notes
Col legno	Hit strings with bow
Con sordino	With mute
Sul ponticello	Bow as near the bridge as possible (produces thin sound)
Sul tasto	Bow over the fingerboard (produces mellow sound)

Tempo

b.p.m.	Beats per minute
Grave	Very slow
Lento	Slow
Largo	Broadly
Larghetto	Rather broadly
Adagio	In a leisurely manner
Andante	At moderate walking speed
Moderato	At moderate speed
Allegretto	Fairly fast
Allegro	(Literally 'merry' or 'cheerful') Fast
Vivace	Lively
Presto	Very fast
Prestissimo	As fast as possible
Accelerando	Getting gradually faster
Rallentando, *Ritardando*	Getting gradually slower
Ritenuto	Holding back
Rubato	Flexible tempo
Tempo giusto	Strict tempo
A tempo, *Tempo primo*	Return to the original tempo

(See also Chapter Nine)

Miscellaneous (a brief selection only!)

8va	*Ottava* (to be played an octave higher)
A Cappella	(In the church style) Unaccompanied vocal music
Ad lib	At the performer's pleasure (i.e. do what you like!)
Attacca	Straight into next section with no pause
Cantabile	In a singing style
Brio	Vigour
Dolce	Sweetly
Divisi	(Of orchestral strings) Divide into two or more groups
G.P.	General pause
Glissando	Rapid slide over keys (piano) or strings (harp)
Legato	Smoothly
Loco	Notes to be played at their normal pitch
Marcato	Marked, accented
Morendo	Dying away
Mosso, Moto	Movement
Ostinato	Frequently repeated
Portamento	Smooth rise or fall of pitch (voice, trombone, violin)
Scherzo	A joke
Segue	Continue without a break
Simile	In similar manner
Sospirando	Sighing
Sostenuto	Sustained
Sotto voce	In an undertone
Tacet	Be silent
Unison	Played together at same pitch
Vibrato	An even fluctuation of pitch (or volume) of a single note
Vivace, Vivo	Lively
Voce	Voice
V.S. (*volte subito*)	Turn the page quickly

SEVENTEEN

Appendix

Pitch Names

It is relatively simple to name a note, but not always so easy to identify its register. If we refer to an F♯, do we mean the F♯ one or two octaves above or below Middle C, and which C is Middle C anyway? The following pitch naming system, using upper and lower case letters plus dashes to signify higher or lower extremes, has been in use in Europe since the 16th century. Also shown is the more modern (and easier to verbalise) American system, which numbers the octaves from 0 to 8.

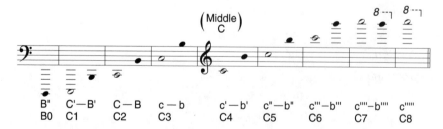

| B" | C'—B' | C—B | c—b | c'—b' | c"—b" | c'''—b''' | c''''—b'''' | c''''' |
| B0 | C1 | C2 | C3 | C4 | C5 | C6 | C7 | C8 |

Instrument manufacturers, though able to agree on the complex details of MIDI specifications, have fallen out over octave numbers, and some companies insist on calling middle C 'C3'. In pipe organ terminology, different octaves are specified by pipe lengths—2', 4', 8', 16' and 32' (high to low respectively). These names still survive in the popular Hammond organ 'drawbar' mechanism.

Indonesian Scales

The Western pitch system of twelve equally tuned semitones (see Chapter One) is far from universal. Other musical cultures, more concerned with melody and rhythm than harmonic modulation, divide the octave into unequal intervals which do not precisely equate to Western pitches. (In fact, these 'untempered' intervals, on first hearing, sound out of tune to Western ears.) Javanese gamelan music (a highly evolved and sophisticated musical form played on gongs, gong-chimes and pitched metallophones) uses a scale called *pelog*–this can be roughly transcribed as:

Javanese
note name: 1   2   3   5   6   4   7

Javanese **Pelog** scale (5- or 7-note)

(The numbers above the pitches are the names now used in Java in gamelan education.) Heard throughout Indonesia, the traditional pelog scale is pentatonic (5-note), with an additional pair of pitches (the notes of '4' and '7') associated with more modern compositions.

Gamelan tuning tends to differ from region to region, and from one instrument maker to the next. Consequently, it is difficult to find two gamelans that are tuned the same! However, there seems to be a convention to tune the note of '6' somewhere between a B♭ and a B. Below are the pitches of a pelog instrument, showing each note's deviation from concert pitch (A = 440) in 'cents'–one hundredths of a semitone.

1	2	3	4	5	6	7
+20	+63	+5	-17	+10	+34	+20

Javanese 7-note **Pelog** scale showing deviations (in cents)
from Western concert pitch

In the equal temperament system, the interval from D to E flat would be exactly one hundred cents—here, it is 143 cents, which makes our 'E flat' nearly three quarters of a tone sharp of the nominal D.

The other Javanese gamelan tuning is the pentatonic *slendro* scale, which divides the octave into five roughly equal intervals—as you can see below, the gaps between the scale steps are 237, 241, 236 and 250 cents respectively! As each interval approximates to two semitones plus a quarter tone, the slendro scale actually sounds quite different from the pitches shown, and the slendro note of '3' is a completely different pitch from the pelog 3. To create some unity between the two tuning systems, instrument makers often tune the note of '6' identically in pelog and slendro.

Javanese 5-note **Slendro** scale

As well as its intervallic idiosyncracies, gamelan tuning adopts a system of 'stretched octaves' in which higher pitches may be 1210 or 1215 cents sharp of their equivalents an octave lower. (A 'tempered' octave is 1200 cents.) To further confuse Western listeners, the instruments also have rather unpredictable, wild-sounding over-tones. Although some digital keyboards offer approximations of the pelog and slendro tunings, the latter consideration makes it virtually impossible to simulate a real gamelan sound using non-gamelan instruments.